MW00824412

MYTHS AND MYSTERIES OF SOUTH CAROLINA

True stories of the unsolved and unexplained

Rachel Haynie

Guilford, Connecticut

Text design: Elizabeth Kingsbury
Layout: Joanna Beyer
Project editor: Gregory Hyman

Map by M. A. Dubé © Morris Book Publishing, LLC

Library of Congress Cataloging-in-Publication Data

Haynie, Rachel.
  Myths and mysteries of South Carolina : true stories of the unsolved and unexplained / Rachel Haynie.
      p. cm.
  Includes bibliographical references.
  ISBN 978-0-7627-5994-1
  1. Curiosities and wonders—South Carolina—Anecdotes. 2. Legends—South Carolina. 3. South Carolina—History—Anecdotes. I. Title.
  F269.6.H39 2011
  398.209757—dc22

                          2010034468

Printed in the United States of America

10 9 8 7 6 5 4 3 2 1

CONTENTS

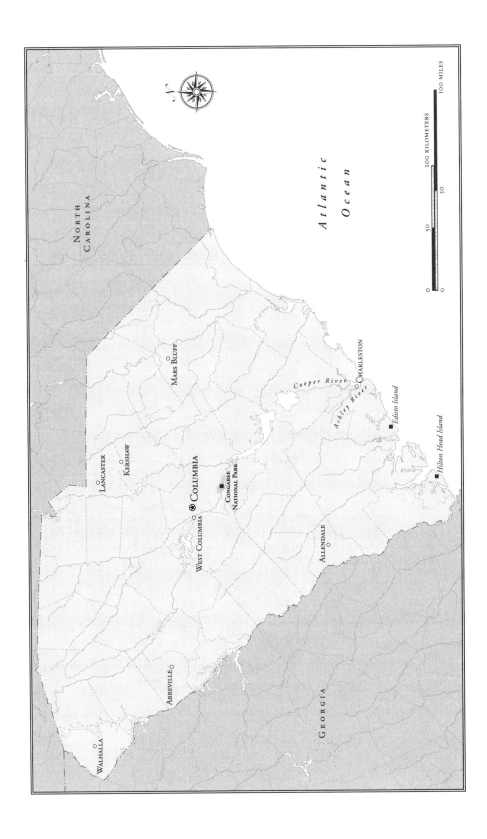

ACKNOWLEDGMENTS

In a state that so reveres its history and is so renowned for its graciousness, finding individuals and institutions to help connect the dots for *Myths and Mysteries of South Carolina* was a delightful introduction, and in welcome incidences, reintroduction.

South Carolina Institute of Archaeology and Anthropology staff members Christopher Amer, state underwater archaeologist, and Dr. Albert C. Goodyear, director of the Allendale Paleoindian Expedition, assisted respectively with the chapters on the state's unique underwater archaeological trail and the Topper site in Allendale County.

South Carolina Department of Archives and History historians Bryan McKown and Patrick McCawley provided helpful information on multiple topics, as did director emeritus Rodger Stroup, in retirement an avid volunteer with the South Carolina Railroad Museum.

Ron Shelton, science curator emeritus, South Carolina State Museum, along with Tom Savage, president of the Paul Rinaldo Redfern Society, provided invaluable continuity for the chapter on Paul Redfern.

Florence City-County Historical Commission Chairman Marshall M. Yarborough recounted information about the accidental atomic bombing in her county, and photographer Tom Kirkland, as well as the principal of Smyle Media, repository for Kirkland's archived images, were also very helpful.

Dr. E. Cantey Haile, a descendant of the family that once owned the Haile gold mine, shared documents from his personal archives, and local historian Louise Pettus referenced material helpful in the development of that chapter.

Instrumental in returning the Hampton silver to South Carolina, Frank Fletcher of Litchfield Beach was aided in that accomplishment by Walker Clarke, president emeritus, South Carolina Archives and History Foundation, and Kay Durham, vintage silver appraiser. Background on the Hampton family was recounted by Janice Bowman, a veteran volunteer with Historic Columbia Foundation.

Art conservator Craig Crawford provided the tip that led to the chapter on Civil War graffiti, and his lead was substantiated by Lancaster local historian Lindsay Pettus, and Ginger Munnerlyn of the Boykin and Munnerlyn architectural firm, headquartered in Camden.

Kristine Dunn Johnson, history curator of the South Carolina Confederate Relic Room and Military Museum, provided support for the chapter on Confederate gold, as did graphic designer Pat Saad.

Of generous support was Martin Crouch, in whose hands are personal archival holdings of his late father Horace Crouch, one of only two Doolittle Raiders from South Carolina. (The other, William Farrow, executed by the Japanese during WWII, was a Darlington native.)

Horseman and breeder David Grant provided a live introduction to marsh tackies on his Darlington County farm, and Fran Rametta, chief interpreter with Congaree National Park, led a nocturnal boardwalk tour for a close look at the fireflies during their peak synchronicity.

Karen Emmons, archivist and librarian for Historic Charleston Foundation, made available pertinent documents relating to Civil War graffiti.

Finally, Dr. John Hammond Moore, James Lamb, William Kaliher, Mickey Burris, and Glenn Neal, along with historians Ray Sigmon and Michael Foley, all contributed the benefits of their knowledge and expertise.

INTRODUCTION

South Carolina has been described by a sage local historian as "one great big cousinry." The entwining of one family's legacies into another's creates a taut tapestry, or a well-primed canvas on which the state's myths and mysteries have been depicted.

Retold as time marches on, many of the state's myths and mysteries change and provide opportunities for a new generation of listeners to gain their own insights. A good example is the Hampton silver that left the state as its heir sought opportunity out west. Much of that silver trove ultimately returned to South Carolina to inspire new questions about domestic life in the Civil War era.

Every South Carolinian represents an arrival. From evidence unearthed at the Topper site in Allendale County, we have learned Early Man, who crossed over on some arctic bridge, favored this place more than 50,000 years ago for its mild climate and its nearness to the navigable Savannah River, whose banks were imprinted by wildlife coming to drink and whose depths teemed with fish.

When the Spanish arrived in search of riches, they purposely or accidentally jettisoned tenacious little horses that survived on the sea islands and along the coast by adapting to whatever environmental conditions nature dished out.

Marsh tackies quietly made their places in the state's history as free work horses and family transportation. Finally, just this year their contributions were acknowledged by a law designating them as State Heritage Horse.

From Alabama, a crew of Confederate innovators skulked into Charleston to commandeer a new stealth weapon that would alter nautical annals. The submarine *Hunley,* fabricated in Mobile, was the first in history to sink an enemy ship in wartime.

Charleston Harbor, where the *Hunley* sunk the blockading USS *Housatonic,* was also the harbor in which Confederate treasurer and entrepreneur George Trenholm applied his considerable business cunning to breaking the strangling nautical blockade keeping essential exports from being offloaded onto South Carolina wharves.

Trenholm's halting steps from Richmond, Virginia, back to South Carolina also trace the path of the Confederate treasure train whose cargo dissipated along the way. The wake of the treasure train is riddled with mysteries that remain unsolved. At one point along its journey through South Carolina, the retreating Cabinet of the Confederacy passed very close to the once-and-again productive Haile gold mine, shut down by federal troops in the early days of the war.

When Union troops were detained in South Carolina—by injury, illness, or capture—they often left indelible proof of their presence on walls confining them. Their military graffiti, a haunting reminder of turbulent times, can still be seen in some revered historic homes and public buildings.

Airspace over South Carolina was the proving ground for a daring young aviator, Paul Redfern. In 1927, only months after Charles Lindbergh made his famous transatlantic crossing, Redfern pioneered the first route to South America, then disappeared forever.

For the Doolittle Raiders, airspace in Columbia was an aerial practice space to ready airmen for a historic first takeoff from an aircraft carrier deck. From the pitching USS *Hornet,* sixteen B-25s roared off for Japan in retaliation for Pearl Harbor.

For an air crew that took off in 1958 from a Georgia base, airspace over South Carolina was where a legendary accident took place. A domino effect of mechanical errors resulted in an atomic bomb pushing its weight out of a bomb bay and smashing into the ground at a Florence County farmstead. The hole created by the bomb remains.

South Carolina's destiny was set, to a definitive degree, by its geography. Its natural harbors helped make it one of the world's most economically important ports, until the discovery—and explanation—of thermal navigation helped Northern shippers understand and navigate ocean currents in ways that eluded Southern ports. Tariffs and other regulatory measures also diverted commerce away from the once-rich ports of call at Charleston, Beaufort, and Georgetown.

Its rivers were colonial-era highways on which plantation owners conveyed their timber, naval stores, phosphate, rice, indigo, and cotton to market. Submerged beneath those rivers are vestiges of those vessels serving still, only now revealing how important the rivers were in those simpler times.

In its craggy northwest corner, geology impervious to engineering breakthroughs that would have linked it by rail to the fast-developing West thwarted the state's commercial development at a critical time in history. Over many decades, even with many leaders cracking the economic whip—including Wade Hampton and George Trenholm—the iron horse never made it through Stumphouse Tunnel. South Carolina never got to share fully in the rewards of westward expansion.

Perhaps the synchronized fireflies that put on a natural light show in Congaree National Park each spring best symbolize the state's myths and mysteries. Before the oceans receded, this bottomland forest was underwater; now it is a richly diverse ecosystem. The fireflies are always there, but not always visible. Their mysteries are only revealed to those with eyes wide open and a willingness to believe.

South Carolina's place in history and unique geography, along with some occasional meetings with fate, have contributed to a growing catalog of myths and mysteries in the Palmetto State. This book provides but a small sample to fascinate native South Carolinians, newcomers, and visitors alike.

CHAPTER ONE

One Mine, Three Centuries

Ernest Thies ladled his secret elixir onto the roots of late summer roses, hung the nicked enamel dipper back up on a nail outside the mining company headquarters, flicked a dried rose hip off his hand-tailored shirt, and went into his office. At 9:15 a.m. a blast from the concentration room sent metal hurtling skyward.

Before the mine workers' shock had time to wear off, Ernest's crumpled physique was rearranged, stretched out on a door, and carefully transported to the big yellow house on the hill. Every doctor in Kershaw County was summoned, but their best efforts were no match for the injuries Ernest sustained. Along with Ernest, who ran the mine, two other workers died that hot August morning. How appropriate: The world's eternal standard of wealth factored into their departure for an eternal resting place!

According to science's best explanation concerning how the universe came to be, gold crystallized in a long vein more than

500 million years ago. Over eons this geologic feature formed in what later became known as Africa. Modern-day technology makes it possible to trace that formation to a gold vein running from present day Virginia to Alabama.

Stories of gold being sought and treasured for its beauty and durability date back many centuries, and in South Carolina, two young boys inspired early legends of the precious mineral.

On his 1540s sweep for riches through what now is northwestern South Carolina, Ferdinand de Soto noticed tribe members in the Native American village of Nepetaca wearing ornate headpieces, armbands, and rings of gold. In keeping with his menacing practices, the Spanish conquistador coerced a young boy to lead his army to the source of the precious metal. This youth, whom de Soto had his priest baptize with the Christian name Peter, traded directions to the source of the gold, or information about how to find it, for his very life. Although Peter held up his end of the bargain, de Soto and company left the area empty-handed. Some believe that gold still awaits discovery. If only the Spaniards had known as they cut their swath through the region! They may have tramped right over some of the most valuable gold deposits in the Southeast.

Fast forward a couple of centuries. In 1799, a young boy just across the state line took home to his father a pretty seventeen-pound nugget he found in a creek near their home. The weight of the rock was the only thing his father noted as valuable, so for three years it was the family's doorstop. Then one day Conrad Reed saw the mineral in a new light and took it to a jeweler, who delighted in informing the German immigrant that his twelve-year-old son had a good eye. The jeweler must have told everybody within earshot about the boy's find because word spread quickly, and soon prospectors were beating a path to the Carolina backcountry hoping their luck would match that of the boy's. The jeweler's loose lips sparked the unofficial start of America's first gold rush, a full generation ahead of California's.

Then in 1802 gold from the same Carolina slate belt was discovered in what then was the Greenville district, but prospectors, intent on their clawing and panning in North Carolina, didn't look up, so it was years later before hunters invaded South Carolina in search of the yellow metal. It was well-bred Southern gentleman Benjamin Haile's discovery of gold on his York District plantation that shifted the prospectors' focus farther south.

Exactly how Haile discovered gold on his place has been the subject of mystery and debate since word of his find spread among his neighbors in 1828. By that time Haile's success had exceeded his father's, who managed to do fairly well in South Carolina after making his way from Essex County, Virginia, with little more than a good name, a mule, and a slave.

Surely Haile would have heard about the Reed boy's find, and, as he walked off his own 1,900 acres, would have kept an eye out for any glimmers of hope his property had the right geology for gold. In one legend Haile spotted signs of gold near his grist mill on Ledbetter Creek. But the story handed down in the Haile family recounts Benjamin Haile reaching deep into his bucket for the last solid handful of daubing mud, pressing it against the chinking of his log cabin, then slogging back over to the nearby stream to scoop up some more of the iridescent clay. With the next handful, meant to fill a gaping crack where rough-cut logs did not fit together perfectly, Haile noticed a definite glint. Just the way the sunlight, filtering through dense hardwood trees, was glancing off the side of the cabin, he probably told himself. But in the next handful of the thick mud, he saw what he was pretty sure were flecks.

Recalling stories of the gold discovered only a few years earlier near Charlotte, no more than a wagon ride north of his property, the plantation owner hurried to finish his task. As soon as he set the last of the chinking in to dry, he began making his way up the streambed searching out the source of that glitter.

He was a smart man, but his education may not have primed him to comprehend that gold deposits underfoot formed within volcanic rocks during the early history of the Piedmont. Northwest of the Fall Line, younger sedimentary rocks of the Coastal Plain abutted older crystalline metamorphic and igneous rocks of the Piedmont creating the right conditions for gold to form. Even today, it is hard to imagine Haile would have known his creek ran right through a geologic feature called the Carolina Slate Belt, beginning in Virginia and ending in Georgia. Panning the stream gravels of Little Lynches Creek, which gurgled through his heavily wooded tract, he soon located the gray-green slate source. From initial placer deposits, he extracted his first gold.

Once Haile's first findings were confirmed, he immediately began setting up a fairly primitive mining operation. Nothing in his background as a planter would have prepared him to set up an operation capable of extracting gold. Perhaps he found someone to help him get started, but if so that person's name has never been revealed.

Luck and chance characterized Haile's business model as he panned the creekbeds' sands and gravel and later moved on to placer mining, each method being about as successful as the other. Placer deposits are signs that erosion or other natural forces have freed the gold from its bedrock and scattered it through sand and gravel. Lode deposits, on the other hand, are bound in masses of rocks such as quartz or siliceous rocks.

His experiment began with a mill having five steel stamps, or pestles, which crushed ore into dust from which he then extracted gold. Even with such rudimentary methods, in his founding year of operation, his success allowed him to ship the first domestic gold sent outside South Carolina to the U.S. Mint in Philadelphia. The year was 1829, and he was being acknowledged as the richest man in the state.

Prospectors, poachers, neighbors, and far-flung relatives wanted a piece of his good fortune, and he couldn't mine it all himself, so as he added to his property holdings, he began leasing land out in fifty-square-foot plots. Some lucky diggers found gold nuggets valued at $300 to $500 in the currency of the day. Rapidly, other deposits were discovered in neighboring counties. Smaller operations dotted topographic maps being read studiously by investors and landowners hoping gold finds would alter their fates as they had Haile's.

He set the benchmark, but once surface mining reached twenty-five feet deep, Haile's productivity hit a plateau, then it dwindled in profitability, even as success surfaced at surrounding mines throughout the area. So, in 1837 Haile brought in a French miner by the name of Gugnot who lived up to his reputation by getting the gold mine into the black, fiscally speaking.

Haile had been well into life when he made his discovery. With his wealth he hired help to do the mining and turned his attentions to public office. He served both as a state legislator and as a trustee of South Carolina College. After he died in 1842, his heirs tramped on with the mine for another generation.

Then, when the Civil War broke out, loss of labor force and shipping difficulties nearly closed down the gold mining production at the Kershaw County site. A mere suspicion the Hailes provided the Confederacy with minerals that might have helped the South prevail was reason enough for the property to go on Sherman's demolition list. Some say copperas (crystallized ferrous sulfate) was secretly shipped out of the area; others say it may have been fool's gold, or pyrite, used for munitions. The Union general ordered all buildings and equipment destroyed as he marched through the area en route to Greensboro, North Carolina, near the war's end.

But buildings and equipment were not all that was lost in that sweep. On their way to the mine, by wagon, were court records from the nearby Lancaster County courthouse. The probate judge there believed the documents would be safer at the mine. Before the load of wills and probate papers reached their intended destination, they were intercepted and destroyed by Union troops.

Devastation to the operation was too great. The Hailes were unable to recover from it and, in 1866, the family lost ownership of the mine. Yankee entrepreneurs tried a variety of mining and management approaches to coax sulfite ore into giving up its gold, but after years of experimentation results were sketchy at best.

The first to try was James Etheridge. The New Yorker also purchased the storied Hobkirk Inn in nearby Camden where the wealthy wintered and, in summer, a steady stream of distinguished guests fanned themselves as they rocked the days away on the broad porches. Under Etheridge's management underground mining methods were attempted for the first time, to little avail. In 1880 a Yankee by the name of Gybbon Spilsbury took over. Within the year the well-funded New York investment company he represented authorized extensive metallurgical testing, implementation of the latest mining operational techniques, and the setup of a twenty-stamp mill. For a half dozen years, the mine averaged production of twenty-five tons of ore a day.

By 1888, the mine's far-reaching reputation helped owners hire away from an out-of-state competitor a brilliant, German-trained mining engineer. Adolph Thies already had extracted potential from mines in Alabama, Georgia, Tennessee, North and South Carolina, Europe, and South Africa. When he arrived again in South Carolina, he brought more than his well-documented expertise with him; he also brought his two sons, Ernest and Adolph, whom he called Dolph.

Soon after setting up at the remote mining community, Adolph perfected a new extraction process. The Thies barrel chlorination process made possible extractions from low-grade sulfide ores. Without resorting to underground mining, his process worked well enough to justify increasing the twenty-stamp mill to a sixty-stamp mill capable of processing one hundred tons a day, although it didn't reach that capacity right away.

New data available from geological surveying, and new procedures, such as diamond drilling, reputedly enabled the mine to produce more gold than any other mine east of the Mississippi River. A narrow gauge railroad conveyed ore from mine to mill. Legend holds that quaint little railroad was built not long after the older son, Ernest, returned from the 1884 World Exposition in St. Louis raving about the fast trains he saw there. No match for the speeds of those trains, the small train lumbering around the property was aptly called the donkey train.

By the time the senior Thies reached his goal of one hundred tons a day, the mine's success was attracting widespread attention, and the well-established mining community had become a destination of the world's foremost mining and metallurgical experts of the period. Visitors from far-flung points of origin found at the mining site a sufficient water supply from a well-stocked pond in addition to a well-stocked company store. There was an official post office, church, and the community had its own doctor. Closing wounds opened by knifings and shootings kept the resident doctor plenty busy. Rare was the man in the village who didn't carry a sharp knife or razor for protection, and Iver Johnson .32s were as common as pocket handkerchiefs.

In a way you could say the camp had its own law enforcement, too. According to prevailing legends, order was maintained by big John Cunningham. He did double duty, as manager of the company store and, on the rare occasion an employee made the mistake of showing up on the premises inebriated, as the village bouncer.

There were no saloons, but residents of the mining community found shadows, nooks, and crannies in which to shoot their dice, deal their poker hands, and dally with "girls of the line."

When one unsuspecting miner slipped into disagreement with one of these rough-around-the-edges women, the argument escalated to a point so volatile he ended up shooting her in the mouth. The female ruffian jumped the goon, beat him, and threw him out into the yard along with his pearl-handled .32.

She wasn't seen around the mine for a short time, but then she reappeared, flashing new front teeth that she swore to anyone who would listen had been shaped out of gold from the mine. Who arbitrated that settlement, and just where the line girl's bridgework was fashioned, remains a mystery.

Far removed from the violence in the story of the line girl's fight and her resulting glinty smile, social life in the Kershaw County mining village offered many forms of diversion you would find in a regular village. Even when no outsiders were on site to impress, there were regular fish fries, picnics, even teas and, in some months with an "r," oyster suppers. Cakewalks were highly anticipated. Yarns about the mining village passed on by the old-timers recalled the sounds of fiddles and harmonicas wafting through the evening air, as well as the infernal whistle on which the donkey train's engineer played his incessant tunes. Guests were entertained at the Thieses' big yellow house on the hill.

Father Thies had been well into his career when he took the top job at Haile's gold mine, so in 1904, when he felt he had accomplished his life's goals, he built a fine home in an up-and-coming Charlotte, North Carolina, neighborhood and retired.

Dolph had long since moved on to seek his fortune at another mine site. Ernest, by then, had gained the experience necessary to keep the operation going at a production capacity comparable to the one his renowned father established. For four more years, the first-born son carried on the legacy and kept the mine's many secrets of success. Some of those secrets involved what fine meats and sauces were placed on his dinner table, whether there were guests that evening or not. Held as closely as a Saturday night card game's winning hand were ingredients in the polish that brought out such a high shine on the two-horse carriage. When his driver conveyed Ernest to his business engagements in town, The Colonel, as he was called by those who reported to him, donned his white linen suit, looped his silk ascot with care, always took his hat, and had at hand his black umbrella.

Part of the managerial legacy the father passed on to his son was to keep very quiet, not only about the proprietary process being used to extract record amounts of gold, but also about how much gold was actually being produced and shipped from the mine. Although detailed records were requisite, they were closely

Gold production never fully recovered after the stamp mill at Haile's gold mine exploded on August 10, 1908.

SOUTH CAROLINIANA LIBRARY, UNIVERSITY OF SOUTH CAROLINA, COLUMBIA guarded. Ernest saw to all such matters personally. Throughout the mining camp, worth and sums were kept mum; on payday the bookkeeper simply hung a red flag in the company store window. One miner did not know what the next miner had coming in his pay envelope. Only Christmas bonuses were paid in actual gold.

And, of course, the ingredients in the elixir Ernest ladled onto his astonishingly lush roses were never revealed. Townspeople on outings often came out to walk the sandy creek banks in search of an exciting yellow find. When the ladies from town stepped out of their carriages and oohed and aahed over his pet blooms, the straitlaced bachelor smiled proudly, tugged modestly at the heavily starched tip of his wing collar, and looked away. Some suspected the mineral run-off from slush filtered over mercury-coated copper plates might account somehow for the particularly vibrant colors. But no one ever knew for sure. The roses also were the source of yet another closely guarded secret at the mine. Ernest concocted a mysterious ointment from his rose petals. Marketed far and wide, Thies Salve worked like magic on just about any kind of skin irritation a person might have.

Ernest had been checking his roses just before the 1908 explosion. One boiler burst itself inside out, its force hurling a smokestack one hundred feet into the air, pulling another boiler loose from its foundation, scattering flues, and raining jagged shards of metal across the village. The searing sound of metal ripping from its construction resonated far and wide. According to legend the roar and whoosh, accompanied by a rumble and quake, was heard and felt as far away as Kershaw. It took occupants of the mining village a few seconds to take in what had just happened to their work and lifestyle, then workers streamed out of the mill and fell to their knees, some crying, some praying, a few cussing. Inspectors on the scene days later blamed a crack in the boiler, gaping enough for a finger to fit through.

Without either Thies at the helm, the mine limped along for a few more years at a good deal slighter capacity than in its earlier productivity, finally closing in 1912. It operated briefly during World War I, and also at the beginning of World War II before President Franklin D. Roosevelt closed all gold mining operations in deference to the war effort. Contemporary attempts to get the mine productive and profitable again have been made, but no recent endeavor has been able to duplicate Ernest Thies's success.

CHAPTER TWO

Redfern's Last Flight

Hollywood's "It Girl" was not accustomed to being stood up. To promote her silent movie, *Wings,* the star's studio sent her to Rio de Janeiro to meet and be photographed with a young aviator being hailed as the Lindbergh of South America. Two days later, when Paul Redfern still had not shown up for the festive street party in his honor, Clara Bow left, and the Brazilian president, also waiting to welcome the pilot and acknowledge a new flying record, went back to running his country.

Redfern never materialized. Traces—real, imagined, and exaggerated—have kept the mystery of Columbia pilot Paul Redfern alive for more than eight decades. His young bride conceded her beloved perished at sea, like other aviators at the dawn of flight. When she closed her eyes, she was still beside her dashing but shy husband in the Stinson Detroiter cockpit, kissing him goodbye before he took off for Rio. It would be a decade later before she fully acquiesced and had him declared legally dead.

Redfern's short life had been devoted primarily to flying. He exhibited signs of being an aviation prodigy soon after his family took up residence in Columbia, South Carolina, where the patriarch, Frederick, accepted a faculty position at Benedict College. The young boy's violin teacher and his classroom teachers confirmed it, and certainly his father recognized the precursors.

First, it was the playable cardboard violin he constructed. Then in 1916, as a sophomore at Columbia High School, he topped that accomplishment with a full-scale airplane. Legend has it the aircraft was of the young man's own design, in a style reminiscent of the day's popular Curtiss Jenny. Metal-trussed, properly bolted, and fully equipped, except for one thing: The aircraft lacked an engine.

His industrial arts teacher recognized its promise by arranging to have the plane erected for exhibition in the gymnasium rafters at the nearby University of South Carolina. With bunting and flags to set it off, the display created quite a stir around town.

The acumen and tenacity he displayed in constructing his first plane, coupled with his teachers' affirmations that he was doing well in all his subjects, earned his parents' reluctant approval when Paul said he wanted to delay high school graduation to get some real-life work experience.

The Army Air Corps took young Redfern on as a production inspector at Standard Aircraft Company's Elizabeth, New Jersey, plant. Little more than a year later, World War I ended and the plant closed, but the teen took his time and logged many more flight hours before finally coming home to satisfy his parents' pleas that he finish high school.

By then, the young man's eyes had been opened to the business of aviation. While away from South Carolina, he got much of his air time barnstorming and performing at aerial shows in a real Curtiss Jenny JN4 purchased with his earnings. He poured his experience into a business venture. The next plane he put together, with help only from a few friends, had the one thing the industrial arts project lacked: an engine.

Redfern got hold of a surplus engine at Camp Jackson (now Fort Jackson) just outside the Columbia city limits, and in 1923 established Columbia's first commercial airport on the site of the present day Dreher High School. According to the company letterhead, Redfern was president and chief pilot of the venture, and B. C. Schoen was business manager. Redfern Aviation Company offered commercial aerial photography, aerial advertising, and passenger carrying.

Legend has it his first landing strip was a former cow pasture at the edge of Columbia's first residential subdivision. From there, Redfern took passengers up for aerial views of South Carolina's capital city.

As the story goes, the first Columbia woman ever to fly went up on a dare. Razzing friends pooled their dimes for her $2 ticket, and goaded her into climbing aboard. When she deplaned, one of her high heels perforated the muslin tautly covering the wood-framed wing of Redfern's creation.

Soon the kick of introducing fellow citizens to the phenom-enon of flight wore off, and Redfern hungered for more excite-ment. Having missed being a World War I flying ace, he began flying at air exhibitions throughout the region, joining the grow-ing lists of barnstormers making headlines and thrilling crowds.

One thrill went too far and became a swoon, then a faint, when Redfern dropped a football dummy from a two-thousand-foot altitude, stunning the unsuspecting air show crowd who had no way of knowing the falling shape was inanimate. For this stunt, and another incident involving buzzing a railroad boxcar, he added jail to his life experiences.

Bent on establishing firsts, he made the inaugural night flight in Columbia on July 4, 1923. Few onlookers were on hand when he took off from an airstrip at the State Fairgrounds about 10:30 p.m. His father illuminated the various roadways over which his adventurous son flew by tying two oil lanterns to the back of his Packard Roadster. From aloft, the young Redfern dropped lighted firecrackers and promotional pamphlets. His mechanic, Daniel Berkman, built a bonfire next to the dirt strip to guide the pioneering pilot's landing.

In 1925 he was working in Toledo, Ohio, as an aerial advertiser. His job? Dropping cigar samples attached to tiny parachutes out over the city. It wasn't long before he married his boss's daughter and brought his bride south. The U.S. Cus-toms Service office in Savannah, Georgia, hired him to scout out moonshine stills from the air. According to the legends, he busted eighty stills during one particularly productive week. For that week's work, his name dominated bureau water cooler talk for a while, but all along, what he really longed for was to have his name associated with a different kind of achievement.

Picking up the *Savannah Morning News* in a restaurant and reading headlines touting Charles Lindbergh's skills and daring whet Redfern's appetite for a record-setting solo flight of his own. Other cities' newspapers headlined other flights, other records. In his mind's eye, Redfern could see his name across a front page.

He signed up for Dole's promotional flight; the Hawaiian pineapple company was sponsoring a nonstop flight from the Golden Gate in San Francisco to Honolulu. When he withdrew from that adventure, his mother was greatly relieved. But then he mustered the nerve to break the news he had something bigger, something more daring in mind.

Savannah dominated the Georgia coast's port commerce, and neighboring ports sought a way to even the advantage and garner larger pieces of that shipping business. So Redfern had no trouble drawing a rapt crowd when he unfurled charts, maps, and a detailed flight plan, and invited down coast business-men to envision with him the prosperity that could be had if a successful trade route were established between Brunswick and South America.

Soon Howard E. Coffin, founder of the resort town Sea Island, Georgia, had formed a business consortium and rallied enough buy-in to support a solo mission to Brazil. Redfern began planning in earnest for a flight that would open up an air route from that ambitious little Georgia port to commercially vibrant Rio de Janeiro. He pictured himself going down in record books for making the first solo flight across the Caribbean Sea.

According to the legend that persists even today, one perk of the expedition reportedly was his getting to choose the airplane he would man in the flight. This much is known for sure: Redfern went straight to Detroit, Michigan, to personally supervise construction of a monoplane at the Stinson Aircraft Corporation. Since he was offered a choice, he chose a Stinson Detroiter SM-1, a high-wing model with a Wright J-5 "Whirlwind" engine, the same type of motor used on "Lucky Lindy"'s *Spirit of St. Louis*. The model also won the 1927 Ford Air Tour.

Besides Redfern's plane, thirty-six others built in the Stinson Aircraft Factory that year also were used in attempts to set world records. Although comparatively large, the SM-1 performed and handled well enough to be set down in what flyers referred to as "the traditional cow pasture," meaning anywhere flat.

At a reported factory cost of approximately $12,000, the plane included, as standard equipment, an inertia-type engine starter, metal propeller, wheel brakes, and wings wired for navigational lights. If he had wished, Redfern could have added pontoons, but did not want the extra weight.

Four back seats were removed to make way for extra fuel. Even today, among those still following this bold adventure, reports conflict as to how much fuel Redfern planned to carry: was it 550 gallons or only 518? The young pilot had calculated the exact amount of fuel he would need to make it to his destination.

Also to be stowed were ten days' emergency supply of food, a two-gallon container of water, and complete survival equipment for either ocean or jungle. As an extra precaution, Redfern was set on packing into the tight space a pneumatically inflatable air raft, a small distilling outfit, mosquito netting and quinine (water), along with a collapsible rifle and appropriate ammunition. And yet a radio, he decided, could not justify its weight.

Among other modifications made to the six-passenger monoplane, Redfern insisted the shades of green and yellow paint on the fuselage match exactly Brazil's national colors. White lettering announced his flight plan, in only three words: Brunswick to Brazil. The plane's name, *Port of Brunswick,* was the other identifier, along with the plane's number NX773.

Stinson himself flew right seat with Redfern to Glynn Islands, another name for Brunswick and Sea Island, and according to legend, tried again in flight to convince the unflappable young pilot that flying alone for two days was more than a man could take. The airplane company's president believed fervently Redfern should take another pilot with him.

Redfern politely declined; a co-pilot would automatically disqualify him from the solo title that was his goal. Lindbergh's Atlantic crossing had taken thirty-four and a half hours; Redfern was certain he would make visual contact with a Guyana lighthouse in the same number of hours. He counted on the favor of tradewinds.

When he arrived in Brunswick, the little town turned out to support him. Locals found in Redfern a worthy hero. The handsome bridegroom's local presence, as he prepared for the slated takeoff, gave surrounding communities along that stretch of the coast time to transfer to the aviator their hopes of gaining worldwide attention for their natural harbor, and ultimately, better revenues. While residents were atwitter at social events surrounding the historic takeoff, Redfern checked and double-checked equipment, maps, and the audacious flight plan.

There were well-wishers, but there also were skeptics. In some camps, trust in Redfern's ability to make it to Rio de Janeiro was guarded. As the local stories go, the confident young pilot offered to deliver U.S. mail to Rio, to demonstrate the viability of the trade route he was blazing. The postmaster on the island nixed that idea. Redfern did take along a couple of envelopes bearing letters of introduction from local dignitaries to Brazilian dignitaries.

Other aviators, weathermen, and astronomers shook their head at the audacity of taking off during hurricane season when there already had been storms, and, perhaps most foreboding of all, Redfern was opting to fly into a moonless night.

The takeoff was delayed for a couple of days by the very winds onlookers worried about. Finally, the headstrong young pilot set low tide on August 25, 1927, for his date with destiny.

A local dignitary brought out onto the hard-packed beach a young lad, James Gould, to shake the pilot's hand and wish him good luck. Redfern had kissed his bride goodbye and warned her not to worry if she didn't hear from him for a while. But when the props cranked up, a strong westerly wind blew the heavily loaded plane seaward, too close to the ocean for Redfern's first takeoff attempt. Thinking quickly, he commandeered a small truck. Onlookers rushed across the wide beach to the plane. In one motion the men lifted the tail of the plane into the bed of the truck and backed down the hard-packed sand far enough to give Redfern an improved shot at a clear takeoff. Then they stood back and held onto their hats.

This time Redfern got the *Port of Brunswick* aloft in a low takeoff that just cleared the mast of a shrimp boat. Five hours later a seaplane spotted him approximately three hundred miles east of the Bahamas. He settled down, found his altitude, reached over, and unwrapped the boxed lunch his wife had packed for him. As he greeted sunrise the next morning, he was somewhere near the Caribbean's eastern islands, if aviation historians have connected the dots correctly. Some speculate he was already disoriented after a sleepless night.

By mid-afternoon a dot on the horizon became a hyphen and soon he could make out the rectangular shape of a freighter. As he approached from the north, he recognized the red field with blue indigo cross of Norway's flag. The *Christian Krogh* was sailing west of Trinidad.

When the hopelessly lost Redfern got close enough to the freighter, he folded down the window and dropped three canisters containing notes to the captain. But just as the canisters began their descent, propeller wash blew the small tins off course. One by one he watched from the air as his plea for help splashed into the water. Transfixed, he next watched the scenario going on below. A courageous crew member dove in, retrieved one of the canisters, swam back to the ship, and ascended the rope ladder his crewmates dropped for him. Throughout the fifty-minute rendezvous, Redfern circled the freighter, his need for help offsetting his concern about fuel depletion. What he had scribbled on a tightly folded square of paper requested that the crew point the ship to the nearest land and wave a flag or handkerchief, once for each one hundred miles.

The captain ordered the ship be pointed toward the Venezuela coast, and the horn blasted twice, communicating that the disoriented pilot was no more than two hundred miles from landfall. Reports, some believable, some questionable, had Redfern flying over Venezuela later that day, but the Norwegian captain and crew were the only eyewitnesses with proof they had actually seen the plane—the canisters and note.

According to alleged witnesses, whose accounts seemed to change with each telling, the pilot in search of renown and Rio passed over the Orinoco Delta in Venezuela. Sailing crafts navigating south along the Orinoco River also claimed to have seen the monoplane flying overhead. Additional sightings near Ciudad,

Bolivia, add to the circuitous nature of the mystery. The story takes on a more somber note with the report by one witness that the plane had a conspicuous curl of black smoke trailing from the nose.

By August 29, 1927, two days after Clara Bow and all of Rio expected to fete him, he was declared missing. There was no sign of him, no word. When the Norwegian freighter docked in New Orleans on September 8 to shift cargo, the cap-

South Carolinian Paul Redfern made aviation history as the first solo pilot to fly from the mainland United States across the Caribbean Sea. Eyewitnesses confirmed he made it to South America, but then he vanished.

tain told reporters what had occurred on the Caribbean Sea. The *Atlanta Constitution* picked up the story.

Back in Columbia Professor Redfern waited in the local daily's newsroom in case information clicked across the ticker-tape. During his waiting days, the desolate father saw news come across the wires that William S. Brock and Edward F. Schlee, taking off from Newfoundland in the *Pride of Detroit,* had completed the first leg of a projected around-the-world flight.

On another day, the professor read dejectedly the news account of Sir John Carlin's flight, with Capt. Terry Tully and

Lt. John Medcalf on board. The three-man crew departed from London, Ontario, in their Stinson-Detroiter, en route to London, England. The front page emblazoned with Redfern's take-off also carried a story on the search for the Dole fliers, six men and a female lost in the Pacific Ocean on an attempted flight from the Golden Gate to Honolulu.

Days turned into months, then years. Redfern's grieving parents finally accepted the hopeless report brought back by explorers they hired to search for any signs of their only son or his plane. Then, in a change of will, they reversed their positions, grasping even tighter the latest thin rumor of a sighting, holding on to empty hope that somehow their fearless aviator was alive.

The aviator's missing status did nothing to diminish his news value. MGM director Jack Conway saw a way to capitalize on Redfern's dubious celebrity. Conway decided to add a subplot based on Redfern's story to the film *Too Hot to Handle*. Playing opposite leading man Clark Gable, Myrna Loy portrayed aviatrix Alma Harding, whose brother is lost in the South American jungles, just as Redfern was presumed to be.

Rumors of Redfern sightings prevailed for another full decade, including one cruel hoax that had him a captive of savages. Another story that broke the family's healing heart all over again reported that he was living in the jungle as a cripple. When Amelia Earhart disappeared in early July 1937, headlines reported on both rumors and the little verifiable information available.

If Redfern's plane went down in the South American jungles, as many continue to speculate, its green and yellow markings might have been easy to spot for the first years after his disappearance. But in time, the fuselage would simply have settled deeper and deeper into the jungle, obscuring the craft from aerial view.

Over the years, at least fourteen documented expeditions have searched for him, and who knows how many other parties have also tried. Explorers have slashed their way through dense foliage, and paddled their way farther up wild Guyana rivers, hoping to come again upon the spot where the trail went cold. Native tribes, seven decades earlier, communicated through an interpreter that a white man fell from the sky and into their midst.

Although Redfern failed in his ultimate goal, he did make history for achieving the first solo flight across the Caribbean. His dreaming big and settling for nothing less make Redfern's legend and its unshakable mysteries as fascinating today as the day he took off on his final flight.

CHAPTER THREE

Nature's Light Show

Night shrouded the queue of hikers who inched cautiously along a raised boardwalk leading through what some call the Redwoods of the East. The canopy of old-growth forest, along with champion trees, was so dense a moonbeam could barely penetrate it.

Their flashlights bobbled modest blotches of illumination into the woods. They were on high alert. Their aspiration that Friday night: to hear, perhaps even see, the owls described by Fran Rametta, the chief interpreter at Congaree National Park. With eerily accurate calls, during the group's brief orientation Rametta had demonstrated the different sounds produced by the barred owl and the barn owl, preparing the hikers to identify the raptors on their wish list that night. Through a sound screen thrown up by thousands of tree frogs and katydids, they listened for that owl call. On the rise of a bluff deep in the Congaree Swamp, eighteen miles away from the state capitol dome, the hikers caught a whiff of wild honeysuckle.

Suddenly, just ahead, a thicket lit up with a spray of tiny lights, like someone had plugged in a strand on a Christmas tree. Stunned, the hikers stopped abruptly. Afraid even a whispered "What is that?" would break the magic spell they were caught in, they froze, forgetting momentarily they'd come to listen for owl hoots. They could only stare.

The lights came on again, then went off. Then on, and when the pale neon yellow lights found their sync, the entire thicket began flashing in unison. The group, whose fondest hope had been seeing a pair of big yellow eyes blink at them from a tree hollow, knew it was beholding some phenomenon of nature. The steady, silent pulsing was hypnotic.

Time was suspended as the night hikers stood on the boardwalk in Congaree National Park, witnessing the forest illuminate in soft light, then go dark again. At first blink, a flicker or two had appeared random, then another spangle flared up. Hikers tried counting to themselves. Once the lights attained a solid rhythm, the bursts persisted for four, five, then six seconds.

The blinks stayed together for five, six, or more cycles, then some of the lights seemed to fall out of the pattern, like musicians in a marching band falling out of step, but in another second or two, the symmetry caught on again. The swath carried on in sync for what must have been nearly another hour. Without speaking, the group stayed in suspended animation.

Eventually, Mother Nature pulled the plug on the light show and the hikers straggled back to the parking lot where Rametta met them at dusk for the evening's guidelines. The awestruck group hunkered around picnic benches, asking their questions in the dark. The interpreter had nearly as many questions as the hikers, but he gave them his most educated guess: "I believe we have seen synchronized fireflies tonight—very rare."

The next morning Rametta turned to his resources. Every glimmer of an answer compelled more questions. Part of him wanted to nail down the facts; after all, he was a man of science by nature. But an inner part of him, perhaps a spiritual part, was willing to leave the mystery veiled, at least some of it. To dissect the question could cut away some of its wonder.

What he discovered confounded him. Rametta learned that there are only a few places in the world where fireflies light up in a syncopated pattern. Southeast Asia had, for decades, been the geographic destination of scientists studying the phenomenon. As fate would have it, the naturalist was in for another surprise: The only other place in the United States where synchronized fireflies had been documented was in Tennessee's Great Smoky Mountains.

Ironically, Rametta had been a ranger at Great Smoky Mountains National Park before coming to what was then Congaree National Monument, now a national park. When he'd left the bears behind and headed to South Carolina's most famous swamp—24,000 acres of old-growth bottomland hardwood forest—the fireflies hadn't been part of the natural scenario, at least not to his knowledge.

Within a short time, his investigations disclosed that synchronized fireflies had indeed been spotted in Tennessee's Smoky Mountains area—by campers at Elkmont Campgrounds. Scientists might have applied the label "Only Anecdotal" to the word-of-mouth reports of families who, for summers on end, had spread blankets in the field at the edge of the forest, sprawled out, and waited to take in the early June light show, but Rametta believed the Elkmont campers had witnessed the same

Pat Saad Designs. Painting by Lucinda Howe

The rich, old-growth bottomland forest in Congaree National
Park attracts fireflies that synchronize their flashing during
the late spring's mating season.

phenomenon the hikers had seen at Congaree. As soon as dark provided backdrop enough for the fireflies to be seen, the beetles seemed to loft from the tall grass like sparks from a campfire.

Rametta wondered: What did the high-altitude Great Smoky Mountains have in common with the low-lying South Carolina floodplain?

Knowing both parks as he did gave Rametta an insider's perspective. He realized both locations had old-growth forest, and both were far enough from city lights to avoid competition from artificial light. Congaree is the oldest stand of old-growth forest in the southeastern United States. Its distance from Columbia and other urban areas assured the cover of darkness the fireflies required for their show.

His curiosity fueled by that first sighting of synchronized fireflies, Rametta continued researching the rarity. It seemed likely that the lighting was a mating signal, but what did it mean that the entire chorus of male lightning bugs flashed its signal in unison—to the entire female population?

Were the fireflies migrating? If so, where had they been and where were they going next? Rametta knew fireflies live in soil for up to two years as glow worms. Once they take wing, they have but three weeks to attract mates and procreate. The interpreter speculated the beetle *Photuris frontalis* had lived among the old-growth woods from birth until maturation.

Perhaps the fireflies had long been the woods' nightlights, but like the tree falling in the forest when no one was around to hear it, there were no witnesses, at least none who would come forward and make a report.

Even though the national monument closed long before dark, Rametta strongly suspected that creatures of the swamp received night visitors. There was plenty of evidence to suggest that poachers and coon and deer hunters slipped in and lowered the mammal population from time to time.

But the only two-legged creatures authorized to be on the site after dark were those who signed up for the owl evening program offered only seasonally, and only once a week. Never before had Rametta seen fireflies flashing in unison, not in all the times he had patrolled the woods at night. He felt certain that dance of light only occurred during the magical mating season, just prior to summer solstice.

Soon he learned the world of science had long been intrigued by the beetle's ability to light. Scientists call it bioluminescence, a natural light that occurs in the cells of certain living creatures, more commonly in those living in the ocean, and even in certain mushrooms.

Fireflies may be the best-known bioluminescent land creature. Bioluminescence benefits organisms by transmitting mating signals, deterring predators via camouflage, and confusing prey being hunted.

As a strategy to prevent misappropriation of water, Cambridge University biologists have introduced genes from bioluminescent jellyfish into potatoes, causing the spuds to glow when exposed to black light if they need to be watered. Medical science is now using synthetic bioluminescence to trace infections' progress, and to assist in AIDS research. But the medical community's interest in fireflies is nothing new. Rametta was surprised to learn that, back in the mid-1950s, Johns Hopkins University researchers paid Baltimore children a penny for every live firefly they brought in. Specimens lit the way to a range of discoveries still being developed.

What makes the fireflies light up is just the beginning of the mystery; numerous theories have been proposed on this matter. What makes them light up in synchrony is the greater puzzle.

In time, Rametta's research led him to Dr. Jonathan Copeland, teaching in the Georgia State University biology department about 150 miles away in Statesboro. In their initial conversation, Rametta learned Copeland already had been to Elkmont, Tennessee, where the professor saw for himself that, indeed, fireflies were synchronizing there.

Before learning he could observe fireflies synchronize at two locations within driving distance of the Statesboro campus, Copeland had traveled to Malaysia and Indonesia to study a different bioluminescent firefly that had been documented there: the *Pteroptyx tener.* Poorly managed tourism in the area coupled with other environmental challenges diminished populations there, but not before Copeland made his observations and notes.

That foray followed two years' study in Savannah where Copeland and his colleagues discovered and ultimately described synchrony in *P. frontalis*. By the following year, drought ended that study. Either the beetle population died out, or the absence of moisture sent the fireflies looking for a more promising habitat.

Over time, Copeland has looked at the rarity of synchronized fireflies from two sides: physiological and behavioral. The biology professor has documented a fair amount more about their behavior while being flummoxed by the function of synchrony.

Returning to Congaree to continue the hunt has become easier, or at least less of a compromise. In recent years the Congaree fireflies have begun setting off their flashes slightly earlier than when their ritual first was witnessed. If Copeland and his colleagues can see Congaree fireflies in late May, they can make it to Elkmont, Tennessee, before the curtain goes up on that show in June.

Synching has emerged as a scientific field and Steven Strogatz, author of *Sync: The Emerging Science of Spontaneous Order* identifies cause and effect. Flashing may well occur if certain conditions are in place: if fireflies have an internal timer, or oscillator, and if they can sense when their immediate neighbors are flashing, and if there's a reason for them to care what their neighboring beetle is doing.

So if it turns out that the female fireflies pay more attention to males who flash first, the race might be on, the ante up. Rivalry could be reason enough for a male firefly to flash slightly before his neighbor. Copeland wants to keep his eye on the female to see how she responds to the come-on.

Mating rituals are among Congaree Swamp's oldest and most evocative mysteries, but there are always new ones. Rametta has solved a few of the mysteries, yet far more still intrigue him. He wonders why tree frogs mate in February, what caused the temporary demise of the bald eagle, what forces are halting the growth of loblolly trees, and why the ivory-billed woodpecker has disappeared. But it is the fireflies that keep him guessing.

While scientists scratch their collective heads over why the fireflies synchronize, Rametta smiles and crosses his fingers that the light shows continue in Congaree National Park. It's a sight he would love to see for years to come.

CHAPTER FOUR

The Tunnel and the Railroad

Stumping up on a wooden leg, an Irish miner hollered his question to anybody within earshot, anybody in Walhalla who would listen: "Has it been kilt intirely?"

"It" was a tunnel through Stumphouse Mountain. This lone miner was the sole survivor of a one-time workforce that once numbered six hundred or more, largely immigrants brought in from Ireland to break northwest South Carolina out of its mountainous imprisonment.

He and his kind had been counted on to open up Stumphouse Tunnel to neighboring railroads, laid and waiting just on the other side. Steel rails offered the state hope of bringing western wealth to the suffering South.

Although work on Stumphouse Tunnel had continued into 1859 with no announcement that funds were drying up again, workers along the line had been laid off. The *Keowee Courier* reported that "foreign laborers" who had settled Tunnel Hill, the mining community that grew, some say, to as many as 1,500, "were breaking off in every direction," bewailing their fate in their mother tongue.

They had appeared on the scene, almost in one fell swoop, able-bodied and motivated. In a short time, many were crippled by mining mishaps or rheumatism. When the money ran out, the workers disappeared nearly the same way they had arrived. It was as though they hobbled into the tunnel, dropped their tools, and somehow vaporized through solid granite.

Tunnel Hill, the mining community where they had hunkered down, brawled, and then been forgiven, became a ghost town. The only trace any of their lot had been there were graves over which Father O'Connell once made the sign of the cross, but tombstones in the Catholic graveyard bore no names.

When the picks and shovels grew silent, work had progressed to within one thousand feet of daylight. Prosperity awaited just on the other side of the crystalline bedrock. Construction to link the upper northwest corner of the state with neighboring states' railways faced about as many fits and starts as the belching steam engines that inspired the protracted project.

Now the Irishman posed his question. Was this yet another work stoppage waiting for the tourniquet of money to relax again, or was the pet project of the state's wealthy and influential being fully abandoned?

It seemed to him the miners were the literal end of the line. Stumphouse was by far the toughest of the final three tunnels whose opening could make reality of entrepreneurs' railroad dreams, already several decades removed. Middle and Saddle Tunnels had been difficult, but possible to excavate. The miners were close, too close, this Irishman thought, for the effort to be scrapped now.

By the time miners, mechanics, and laborers were brought in by another in the cavalcade of contractors, a lot of private and public money had bought and paid for both trial and failure. Zeal for the project that some hoped would bring new prosperity from the quick-rich West into the old-moneyed South had dissipated. Few who had made the promise several decades earlier were still around, and if they had remained, investors and other visionaries would have been saddened to see how the plans had fallen apart.

From Ireland to London, London to New York, New York to Charleston, employers had enticed hardworking immigrants to do the job. Although rail spurs had cropped up throughout the state, South Carolina had fallen behind neighboring states in networking its railroads. Would the people of the state ever see what the tracks could do for their economy?

In contrast with northwestern South Carolina, in the Lowcountry where the goal of connecting the port city to inland areas was first proclaimed, the promise was kept and the payoffs held up as incentive to keep laying rail. Both political and geological terrains were much easier to navigate there. The beginning of the Industrial Revolution signaled the end of Charleston's reign as a commercial center of national consequence. After cotton prices began slumping in the 1820s and populations ventured to far-flung new frontiers, the New World's one-time richest city was rocked by an alarming economic recession. Yet Charleston was adamant about retaining her prominence, and resolved to construct her own avenue to the West.

As Charleston merchants vehemently sought means to revitalization, sibling rivalry surfaced among other cities also vying for shares of the wealth pouring in through natural and man-made conduits—first rivers, next canals, and then railroads.

Although New York already was in a commercial league of its own, buoyed substantially by the opening of the Erie Canal, other cities watched, green-eyed with wonder as wealth funneled through from West to East, and into New York harbor. Hundreds of miles away, this flow influenced Charleston transportation and shipping, even from that great distance.

Because maritime traffic between New Orleans and New York had to navigate hazardous passages around the Florida peninsula, and insurance rates between Charleston and New York were favorable, the venerable port city saw itself as economically advantageous to merchants shipping to the north. Yet Charleston felt even more acutely its proximity to Wilmington, North

Carolina, and Savannah, Georgia. It was no longer willing to gamble its prosperity only on natural harbors.

Along with a plan to link the Savannah and Tennessee Rivers with a canal, Charleston city fathers were open to more futuristic solutions. If Charleston took its cue from the mother country it broke ties with less than a century earlier, it might right its financial vessel.

Throughout Europe, but especially England, the concept of steam locomotion was altering transportation, and therefore commerce. Nineteenth-century Charleston business leaders and other investors believed following suit would help restore the port city to its earlier eminence as a commercial center.

A rail route from Charleston to Louisville and on to Cincinnati first was proposed as early as 1827 by E. S. Thomas, then of Cincinnati, but formerly of Charleston. For his proposal to fall upon the right ears took a full year. At an 1828 city council meeting, speakers lamented that Charleston's "landed estate has depreciated, talent has sought employment elsewhere, houses sit tenantless, and grass grows uninterrupted in some of the city's business streets."

Both a canal and rail route to Augusta made it possible to divert shipments away from Savannah, Charleston's staunchest competitor. Charleston city fathers lobbied the South Carolina legislature to charter the South Carolina Canal and Rail Road Company to explore the viability of a system that would connect Charleston with inland merchants.

To strengthen this bid, Charleston ordered from the West Point Foundry of New York the first steam locomotive built completely in the United States. The engine arrived by packet ship, disassembled, at a Charleston wharf in October 1830, was named the *Best Friend of Charleston,* and made its inaugural run on Christmas Day.

Regular passenger service along a six-mile, in-town demonstration route earned praise for this progressive form of transportation that sped along the shiny steel rails at a rate of speed previously attainable only by a strong and experienced horse—fifteen to twenty-five miles per hour. Within five months Charleston's economy was improving and a second locomotive was ordered, this one named the *West Point,* for the foundry where it was created.

However, a little more than a month after engine two came on line, the *Best Friend* suffered a boiler explosion. What brought the tragedy about is still a mystery.

Although those who might have witnessed it were inside the train, some allegations point to a fireman sick and tired of hearing the whistle of the steam pressure release valve. His solution, as the speculation goes, was to wedge a chunk of lumber over the safety valve, then sit on it. When pressure built up, the boiler explosion killed the fireman, scalded the engineer, and obliterated the train, hurling metal fragments into the South Carolina countryside.

But the tragedy did not dim the public's perspective on railroading. Six locomotives, including the *Phoenix*—fabricated from the *Best Friend*'s remains—were operating by the time delegates arrived in Asheville for a September 1832 regional convention whose goal was promoting a westward railroad line traversing the valley of French Broad River.

By the time the first track was completed in 1833, the railroad was the longest under single management in the world. Passengers and freight were conveyed to and from Charleston to Summerville, Branchville, Blackville, and Aiken, with Hamburg as its terminus. Elias Horry, president of the chartered South Carolina Canal and Rail Road Company, used the occasion marking the completion of 136 rail miles to urge the ongoing support of the people.

While rails linking South Carolina's districts were coming on line, pockets of investors kept their eyes on regional prizes. Their appetites for profits had been whetted by the success of local rail ventures. Longing for commercial conduits between South and Midwest, entrepreneurs attended an 1835 fall meeting in Cincinnati where consensus was easily reached that the Charleston/Louisville/Cincinnati rail route was still desirable and practical.

Robert Y. Hayne, who had previously served both as a U.S. senator and governor of South Carolina, had become a passionate proponent of the railroad. The talented orator spoke at the convention with the same conviction that characterized his 1830 Congressional debate with Daniel Webster.

"The period has now arrived when work can no longer be neglected, without a criminal supineness and fatal disregard of all our best interest, as well as duties with which we owe ourselves and posterity," Hayne said.

Conditions of the charter approved that same year called for the other three states through which the railroad was to pass to be granted similar charters. States participating were stopped for thirty-six years from permitting construction on any parallel railroad within twenty miles of the existing track. Also, the railway operation was exempt from paying taxes in those states.

In 1836 Governor George McDuffie recommended the General Assembly approve funds for surveying the proposed route. Although a match of approximately $10,000 was requested of North Carolina and Tennessee, only $5,000 from Tennessee ever was made available.

On July 4 of that year, 380 delegates representing Indiana, Ohio, Kentucky, Virginia, North Carolina, South Carolina, Georgia, Alabama, and Tennessee met in Knoxville to promote the proposed railroad. While South Carolina and North Carolina were enthusiastic, other states were lukewarm. Only some portions of the projected route were to traverse North Carolina, and Georgia had its own railroad to the west in the works.

Hayne, who later would become president of the Charleston Louisville and Cincinnati Railroad, chaired the convention. His national experience provided him the perspective to recognize signs of impending rupture between North and South. In his speech at that gathering, he urged "forming lasting unions between West and South by binding them in mutual sympathies and common interests, breaking down all barriers which now divide them and causing the streams of commerce to spread its benign and fertilizing influence through the region which wants only this: to become the fairest portion of the globe."

The general public did not share Hayne's vision. Less than half the $11 million needed to make the railroad a reality was invested. By 1839 all construction beyond Columbia had stopped.

Some groups favored the railroad, while others were against it. As a progressive initiative, landowners along the routes so favored the coming advancement they not only granted rights of way, they also offered the muscle of their own slaves to speed work along. Conversely, districts not showing up on maps indicating where rails would be laid were vehemently against state money being used as spikes for this venture.

Perhaps the highest profile proponent of the railroad was John C. Calhoun, but only if it ran where he thought it should go. When the notion of a rail connection was no more than a gleam in the eye of visionaries, the raw-boned leader walked off the entire tract near Rabun Gap, searching for a chink in South Carolina's mountains through which a tunnel might be excavated most efficiently.

The region of Rabun Gap represented a relatively low place through the Appalachian chain in northeast Georgia, and Calhoun's promotion of it brought the less daunting stretch much attention as a potential route. Interest was heightened when gold was discovered at Dahlonega, Georgia, to the west.

Convinced that the spot he found was the right one, Calhoun pushed his agenda. That his one-time protégé Hayne took another position, suggesting the rail line follow the contour of the French Broad River, so infuriated Calhoun he resigned from the railroad board.

Just when the two split on this matter is part of the railroad mystery in South Carolina. Hayne, who supported earlier initiatives with Calhoun, had stepped down from his U.S. Senate seat to make room for the latter after the U.S. vice president resigned in response to President James Monroe's appointing Kentuckian Henry Clay Secretary of State. Calhoun went back to the U.S. Senate and Hayne came home and became mayor of Charleston where railroading was at a fever pitch.

According to legends tracing the railroad's developmental twists and turns, Calhoun's influence is one strategic reason why the line never was completed. Calhoun considered it a personal triumph that railroad development stopped in Columbia, even after Hayne died suddenly of a fever in 1839 while in Asheville.

Attracting public capitalization had always been part of the board of directors' plan, but as the project wore on and costs rose, the company was unable to attract enough support to keep pace with the costly development.

Spartanburg thought it had a better chance to route the railroad up the valley of the Broad River. Some feared the railroad would make the port city, already the envy of other municipalities, too important. There were few takers on the port city's claims that a stronger Charleston would benefit the entire state.

Over the years when the General Assembly approved price tags for the railroad's development, it attached strings: liens and stipulations, some of which made cultivating private funding impossible. When legislators would no longer approve additional funding, stockholders told the State either to put up money or get out of the way.

Proponents of the railroad expressed particular disappointment that the needs of the Blue Ridge Railroad (as it was then called) had been ignored in favor of approving funds to build the State House, an outlay many thought extravagant. In an editorial the *Keowee Courier* invited the state "to follow more than one idea, and carry out more than one enterprise at a time." After the State entered into and encouraged this railroad venture, one eloquent proponent said, "if the proposition is made to abandon her work, would it not be a declaration that she cannot pursue that which she originally intended?"

The project stretched out over so many years that investments were made only timidly, and public apathy set in, although townspeople were more than willing to dress up and come to picnics celebrating even a small milestone. Meanwhile, a cavalcade of contractors had come and gone, some corrupt to the core, some well intentioned, at least at the time they signed their names on the binding agreements.

Over three decades investors, politicians, and other leaders bickered and lobbied for their individual agendas. Their greed and corruption prevented legislative consensus from being reached, so no funding was approved to keep the project on track to reach the other side of the mountain.

In 1838 a fire destroyed more than $3 million worth of property in Charleston; that, along with general economic stagnation, led financial institutions to call in payments which were due.

By the time stockholders gathered for their 1840 annual meeting, all hope of laying track across or through the mountains had been abandoned.

A decade later the dream of piercing the mountains and releasing the flood of wealth from the West was revived. But by then the traffic flow via rail already was well established, and making commercial inroads would be more difficult than in the days when the mode was new.

Approximately one-third of Stumphouse Mountain Tunnel was complete and backers expected the remaining portion could be finished within three years. On April 8 that year, completion of thirteen miles from Anderson to Pendleton was celebrated by a picnic attended by five thousand people.

Pat Saad Designs. Photo by Ron Shelton.

Investors and other South Carolina leaders never got to see
their vision of a train traversing Stumphouse Mountain tunnel.
More than a century later, it remains a tunnel to nowhere.

When the legislature voted to withhold continued public
support for the Blue Ridge Rail Road, all work came to a stop.
Elected officials shrugged off mockery, leading the *Charleston
Mercury* to publish its opinion in an editorial. "Too many of the
state's leaders are measuring the impact of the railroad by the
little pocket rule of immediate dividends." Perhaps those who
represented their constituents under the dome in Columbia had
heard states' rights rumblings and were squirming.

So the Irish miner's question went unanswered; no one
really knew whether the project was "kilt intirely." Contractors
walked off the job when they heard there would be no more

money, and the board of directors had exhausted its lobbying efforts. The General Assembly voted down the budget.

When the miners shuffled out of drafty shanties their last morning, and entered shafts filled with sulfur and black powder fumes before vanishing from Tunnel Hill, they took nothing with them.

According to local lore, some immigrant miners followed the railroads west, some stopped off in Dahlonega in search of gold, and some fought in the Civil War.

Over the years several more attempts were made at reviving the railroad, but no one has ever seen a light at the end of Stumphouse Tunnel. It is still dark inside and leads nowhere.

CHAPTER FIVE

Legendary White Lines

Another tuft of broken rope on the new runway! Muttering "What's this about?" to himself, Russell Maxey began to pick up the fragments and stuff them into his work pants' pocket. On the short drive to the hardware store up the road from the air base, he tried to piece together clues as to what he was seeing. He trudged to the counter, shaking his head.

The clerk said, "Back so soon? What d'ya need so much rope for, anyway?" Maxey leaned across the counter and handed the clerk a piece of paper with the base purchase order number and said, "Doggone if I know. Just doing what I'm told. I requisition it, they cut it up. I find little pieces of it scattered on the runway and all along the apron."

As he was leaving, he warned the clerk over his shoulder, "Probably going to need more white paint next time I come in." Maxey wedged the huge spool of rope into the passenger seat of his car and rumbled back to the air base.

He had been ordered to paint lines on the brand new runway at Columbia Army Air Base to very specific dimensions. The guy putting white lettering and identification numerals on the new water tower noticed it first: "From up here, looks like the deck of a ship."

Maxey wasn't military; he was an engineer with the U.S. Corps of Engineers, but he obeyed the base commander's orders nevertheless. The scuttlebutt was that orders to paint the white outline had come directly from Lt. Col. James Doolittle. The colonel had no official standing on the base, but his reputation as a fearless flyer and compelling leader inspired Maxey to comply without question. Maxey knew for a fact Doolittle had been on the base the day before, adding credence to the rumor that the mysterious orders, issued days earlier, had come down through the chain of command, starting with the renowned aviator.

Maxey had been on the airfield project beginning with its 1940 inception; the Columbia native tried to sort through what little he knew about the motivation behind the airfield's construction. Along with forty-nine other engineers with the U.S. Corps of Engineers and hundreds of other civilians, Maxey had been clocked in nearly nonstop to convert fallow, but level, fields into a county airport.

In its most ambitious aeronautical expansion program to date, Congress had approved $700 million to be invested over six years for improvement of the country's air defense capabilities.

A nationwide grid of 250 strategically located airfields was to be developed, sites that could easily be converted for military use if international tensions boiled over and America went to war.

Just weeks earlier, residents around the state's capital had taken off from the new field in commercial planes. The U.S. Corps of Engineers' Major Charles Gableman announced on December 2, 1941, the airport would be ready for units to be assigned to it within the week. The Lexington County Air Field was to be one of the largest in the Southeast, with capacity for up to two hundred planes.

Now all departures and arrivals would be made by crew members who had joined the Army Air Corps in their respective states. They had taken basic training at one of many bases that had sprung up quickly around the country, just as this base was emerging. Now those crews were training for combat. The airfield's fast transition from a civilian field to military base was made December 8, the very day after the Japanese bombed Pearl Harbor.

Maxey had many unanswered questions. What was Doolittle doing at the air base? Why did he want the outline of a ship painted on one of the brand new runways, and why a configuration of only five hundred feet?

Being away from his regular duties to buy more rope threw the engineer behind, so it was nearly dusk when he left his desk. Inquisitive about the thrum of B-25 engines, audibly revved up, Maxey followed the sounds to the same runway that bore his white lines. What he witnessed was even more baffling.

There, straining against the power of an earth mover that, earlier in the day, had smoothed layers of soil and concrete onto the third and last runway, a B-25 groaned at the end of rope Maxey had procured. Just when the plane had stretched the tether to its absolute tensile capacity, the rope was cut and the craft lofted almost straight up. Maxey whipped off his cap and scratched his head. What did his hero Doolittle, the aeronautical mastermind, think would be accomplished by such training? His answer was weeks in the offing.

On February 3, Doolittle flew into Columbia Army Air Base again to ask for volunteers for a top-secret mission. His arrival on this base had been predestined by decisions that had taken place in and near the nation's capital since December 7, the Day of Infamy. Columbia Army Air Base was in the right place at the right time. And Maxey's lines were not the first to factor into this historic turn of events.

If an astute submarine captain had not noticed similar lines on a deck at a naval base runway, the painting of lines on the Lexington County runway might never have been ordered. When Francis Low's plane was departing the Norfolk base where he'd just inspected the Navy's newest carrier, he looked out and saw Navy pilots practicing short-run takeoffs from a carrier deck. Admiral Ernest King's directive was on his mind: "Find a way for the U.S. to bomb Japan." He knew Navy planes were not the solution, but he wondered what other planes might take off from a carrier deck—within bombing range of Japan.

Low had an idea, and Admiral King brought in the best aeronautical mind he could muster to see if it would work. Lt. Col. James Doolittle's office was right down the hall. Questions were fired off and answered at record-breaking speed.

What plane could take off from a carrier deck? Wingspans and takeoff requirements were considered. The only plane the Army had that might work was the B-25, with a wingspan of sixty-seven feet—if its weight could be reduced to take on additional fuel tanks. The Mitchell bomber, named for an aeronautical pioneer, could fly the low altitudes the best military minds knew would be essential to escape detection, avoid anti-aircraft fire over land, and increase bombing accuracy. The number of planes that could strike back at Japan was determined by how many could fit on the carrier deck.

Next, where were there crews with the extant experience to fly that many B-25s? That answer was easy: the 17th Bombardment Group out of Pendleton Air Base, consisting of the 34th, 37th, and 95th squadrons, as well as the associated 89th, were flying anti-submarine watches off the Oregon coast.

Doolittle took the first B-25 to Wright Field in Dayton, Ohio, and initiated modifications that would lighten the craft adequately to allow for a two thousand pound payload. Other planes were to follow for the same modifications. Practice runs on auxiliary fields had gone smoothly, so Admiral King ordered the new carrier out about thirty miles off the Atlantic coast so Navy pilots could practice short-run takeoffs.

On February 1, Lt. Col. William C. Miller of the 17th received orders to transfer the group under his report at Pendleton Air Force Base in Oregon to Columbia Army Air Base where the only operational units of B-25s were up and running. Miller was also told to filter word throughout the group that, once in Columbia, volunteers would be invited to take part in an extremely hazardous mission, one that would require the highest levels of secrecy.

Some of the airmen were ordered to make a mid-continent stop in Minneapolis en route to Columbia Army Air Base. About twenty planes were flown to an aeronautics factory there and, to the airmen's surprise, B-25s were being modified with additional fuel tanks to nearly double the capacity of gas that could be carried from 646 gallons to 1,141 gallons.

De-icer boots were being screwed into the wings, bomb shackles were put in place, and landing flares were relocated forward of the rear armored bulkhead. Cameras were being attached to a few planes. And the biggest mystery of all was that wooden broomsticks, painted black, had replaced .50-caliber machine guns that usually protruded from the tail.

Crews of the 17th thought they were merely swapping anti-sub lookouts along the Pacific coastline for the Atlantic, although they wondered about being based so far inland. Regardless, after months in the dreary Northwest, the airmen looked forward to a South Carolina spring. They counted on their fellow crewman Horace "Sally" Crouch to show them around his hometown.

By February 3, all squadrons had reported to Columbia Army Air Base. Some airmen had already been practicing short-run takeoffs. Despite rumblings and rumors, they all were surprised when Lt. Col. James Doolittle showed up in person. For many of the airmen, their regard for Doolittle was the reason they had wanted to fly in the first place. When he invited them to become part of a mission very important to the country, one sure to be highly dangerous, he could tell them little of what they could expect. That they would be out of the country for an unspecified period of time was about all they learned.

One airman who had been on night duty and was a couple of minutes late to formation arrived just as everyone's hand was going up. "What are we voting on?" he asked the airman standing next to him. "Just raise your hand: you'll want in on this!" All crews volunteered to go. From them, twenty-four full crews were picked.

For the remainder of February, airmen practiced short-runs, lifting off before reaching the lines Maxey had painted, but they still couldn't guess what mission could be important enough for James Doolittle himself to be giving the orders. Paint from the white lines had begun to chip off, helped along by late winter rains, when new orders swept through the base. By March 1 airmen who had volunteered for Doolittle's mission were off to another base, where they continued training in secret.

Eglin Air Force Base, just outside Pensacola, Florida, was the U.S. Army Air Corps' proving ground, with seven or eight fields away from the main strips where airmen demonstrated they could take off and land in a mosquito-infested swamp without rousing the curiosity of the citizenry. Crews thought surely they would get some time to relax on the wide white beaches just across the highways, and a few did pay with goose bumps for an early swim in the Gulf of Mexico, but their training regimen demanded most of their time.

The crewmen finally learned more in early March when Doolittle showed up again. They knew he had been the mastermind of the mission; now he told them he also would be leading it. Although he had been told in Washington he was valued too highly as a staff member to take the risk, with some fast talking and shrewd political maneuvering he managed to get permission to lead the group.

In his briefings with the chosen crews, Doolittle was forthright. "It is inevitable that some of the ships will fall into enemy hands," he said. Unwilling to presume that every American serviceman calculated risk as astutely as he did, he offered again an easy out to anyone who wanted one. There were no takers. Doolittle stressed again the need for utmost secrecy. "If anybody outside this group gets nosy, get his name and give it to me; the FBI will find out all about him."

The crew figured as long as Doolittle was with them, whatever he wanted them to do, they would do. Some called him lucky, but "I have never taken an uncalculated risk" was Doolittle's mantra, and the crew knew of his cross-country records, speed trophies, and stunt-flying achievements. Nearly as well known as Charles Lindbergh in aviation circles, he had even developed a high octane fuel that allowed planes to fly longer on one tank.

As the crews trained rigorously, Doolittle was back and forth to Washington. In the early days of planning for this vital mission, many things that could have thwarted the effort fell into place easily: the choice of airplane, an experienced crew, a secure place to train. But now his luck was tested to its limits, much as the rope holding back planes at Columbia Army Air Base. Numerous problems developed: fuel tanks leaked, gun turrets jammed, carburetors threw themselves out of factory-set adjustments, hydraulic systems developed glitches.

To push through the planes' modifications, he had to make a phone call and request intervention from the top to emphasize the work was top priority. Then Russian leader Joseph Stalin refused President Roosevelt's permission for American planes to land in the Russian seaport Vladivostok, the ideal refueling spot, only six hundred miles from Japan. Doolittle didn't know the Chinese had also tried to delay the mission, but the ally's apprehension had to be ignored; the wheels already were in motion. America wouldn't turn back.

Before March elapsed and long before they could work on suntans, the crews were ordered to McClellan Air Force Base near Sacramento, California, where they continued training as secretly as possible, including runway work at a nearby airstrip,

Willows, and last-minute engine adjustments at the Sacramento Air Depot. They quickly moved down coast to Alameda where the B-25s were hoisted onto the deck of the USS *Hornet,* positioned closely, tied down for safety, and tarped for security. Once again, painted lines were precursors to the making of history.

The *Hornet,* in convoy with Task Force 16, comprised of Vice Admiral William Halsey's carrier, the USS *Enterprise,* a fuel tanker, escort cruisers, and destroyers, had steamed to within one hundred miles of their strategic launch point. Once again, white lines were painted, this time to mark where both the left wheel and nose wheel should set, leaving six feet as insurance. Each bomber carried two demolition bombs weighing five hundred pounds each, to be followed by a thousand-pound incendiary bomb.

In a motivational ceremony, Japanese "friendship" medals were affixed to the tips of some of the bombs. The tokens had been given to American military personnel only months before Japan bombed Pearl Harbor. As Doolittle attached the first one, a roar of patriotic thunder followed his sarcastic announcement: "Your government has asked that you politely return these."

Final briefings were given. The planes had been rocked to rid gas tanks of bubbles, and the ship's doctor had issued each crew two pints of medicinal rye, emphasizing the whiskey's antiseptic qualities. Expecting they'd be taking off in ten hours, the crew had stowed in their planes items not likely available in China: razor blades, toothpaste, candy bars, and cigarettes.

Warned about China's primitive sanitation, Columbia's Horace "Sally" Crouch stashed rolls of toilet paper in his bag. Another airman insisted on taking his wind-up phonograph with him; his plane was fully packed when he realized his cake tin of records hadn't been stowed, so he pleaded with a buddy to secure his treasure under the crew seat of his plane.

Absent from all bags were personal items that could tie a crewman with any base on which he'd served, any place he'd been, anyone he loved. Diaries, journals, and photographs were secured in a box to be returned to stateside later.

The planned takeoff was timed to position the planes over Tokyo after nightfall. That schedule gave the crew one more chance for some sleep. Suddenly, a Japanese picket boat, disguised as a fishing boat, appeared in the scope of a crewman on watch. That the task force had been spotted was confirmed immediately when a Japanese radio message was intercepted and interpreted. Roiling waves and pea-soup visibility delayed for nine full minutes the USS *Nashville*'s sinking of the Japanese boat.

So ten hours earlier than planned and 170 miles farther out than fuel had been calculated and allocated, the *Hornet*'s klaxon blared: "Army pilots, man your planes!" and sixteen B-25s took off for Tokyo. It was the first and only time Army Air Force bombers launched for a combat mission from a Navy carrier.

Throughout a three-hour offensive, targets hit in broad daylight—not cover of darkness as planned—included key industrial sites in Tokyo, Yokohama, Kobe, and Nagoya. But

White lines, like those painted on a Columbia air base runway, guided the Doolittle Raiders as they took off from the deck of the USS *Hornet.*

then instead of fleeing on across to China in daylight, crews were forced to navigate their ally's eight thousand foot mountains at night. The only plane that came down on its tricycle wheels landed in Russia; America's ally detained the crew for more than a year. All other planes were lost, crew members scattered.

On April 20, the day following the raid, newspapers around the world used their biggest headlines to verify the secret mission's success. Despite Japan's public claim that the bombing had done little damage, international headlines roared that Doolittle's Raiders had done to Japan what the island nation's propaganda machine said was impossible. Sixteen B-25s, including ones Maxey watched lift off before reaching his white line, launched from the pitching deck of an aircraft carrier more than four hundred miles off the Japanese coast to rain fury on the country that bombed Pearl Harbor.

Finally, the engineer back in Columbia had his answer. The B-25s at Columbia Army Air Base had been practicing short-run takeoffs so they could take off for Tokyo from the deck of an aircraft carrier.

From then on, pride by proxy pervaded the Lexington County air base. By transference, even airmen yet to report to Columbia Army Air Base dared to speak their names in a sentence that also referenced Lt. Col. James Harold Doolittle. The legendary aviator's huge shadow had been cast across the growing air base that took on the persona of the Doolittle Raiders.

The guts and guile, skill and secrecy of that mission permeated operations in Columbia from then on. Although the spirit of courage and oneness of purpose that characterized the Doolittle Raid was indelibly imprinted on Columbia Army Air Base, the telltale white lines ultimately disappeared from the hardtop.

Months later, some of Doolittle's crew members were still unaccounted for. Those who made it through the Chinese underground and were repatriated began the arduous process of detailing their stories in official reports.

On Friday, June 19, 1942, Doolittle was back on Columbia Army Air Base to whip up morale by discussing plans to speed up the operational training unit with the outfit's officials.

Then recently promoted Brigadier General Doolittle told pilots stationed at the South Carolina base their fellow members of the 17th Bombardment Group had "acquitted themselves superbly on the dangerous volunteer mission. They are the finest group of men I ever served with."

Doolittle returned to Columbia in May 1980, for the dedication of a U.S. Army Aviation Flight Facility named for him. Its location? The same spot where he invited volunteers for the historic mission that took his name—only the airfield had become Columbia Metropolitan Airport.

Doolittle's Raiders returned to Columbia in 1992, 2002, and 2009 for their reunions, begun by their leader at the end of the war.

CHAPTER SIX

Carolina Silver in the South Pacific

Frank Fletcher left his wife alone just long enough to take care of one quick errand. The temperature in the Fiji Islands that January afternoon had already reached the high 80s, so when the couple left the craft bazaars and spotted a McDonald's with a banner touting its air conditioning, Frank suggested Jodie wait there in the cool.

He returned in only a few minutes to find his gregarious wife, thousands of miles from home, chatting with a resident of the capital island, Suva, like the two were long-lost friends. Fletcher was not prepared for what came next. With introductions he was quite surprised to learn the new friend had historic ties to South Carolina. She was the great-great granddaughter of Wade Hampton III, Civil War general, U.S. senator, and governor of the state.

The conversation had to end soon so the couple could return to the cruise ship anchored nearby. As they got up to leave, their new friend, Barbara, rose from the tiny table at the same time; she was expecting evening guests and had preparations to make. Before good-byes were said, the two women exchanged contact information and promised to correspond. Jodie said, "Please tell your mother I would be happy to try to help her, if ever she wishes."

Throughout their years together, Fletcher had admired Jodie's ability to make friends easily. He viewed her extroversion as a gift, one she was oblivious to having. He was a little baffled, though, by the level of enthusiasm Jodie was displaying after the chance meeting with this Fijian resident. Sure, she was a genetic link to one of their state's most revered heroes but, after all, the woman lived on Fiji. Had she ever even been to South Carolina?

Over the next few minutes, as the couple made their way back to the waiting cruise ship, Jodie revealed why she was so intrigued by the Hampton descendant. During their short conversation, her new friend had entrusted Jodie with a family secret: Her mother had inherited a cache of antique silver that, in the preceding century, graced Wade Hampton's tables. Fletcher's jaw dropped.

According to the family story just told to Jodie, the silver left South Carolina when Wade Hampton III's youngest son Alfred went west to begin his career; as his career advanced, he moved farther west, finally to California. Two generations later his only daughter's daughter moved from California to Australia, taking the silver with her. That Aussie was the new friend's mother.

Now the retired business executive quickly calculated the odds of running into the great-great granddaughter of Wade Hampton III in a McDonald's in the Fiji Islands—and, on top of that, the stunning coincidence: the woman's family possessed a cache of silver that had been away from South Carolina for at least a century.

Although their new friend gave no details as to what time periods in the Hamptons' lives the silver represented, Jodie knew her state history. And as a collector of antique silver, she knew any pieces owned by any generation of this family would be a treasure trove.

The fascinating story had both Fletchers' mental wheels turning. How had the silver survived the Civil War? Was it ever buried, as other legendary family silver in the South had been? Had it been wedding gifts or commissioned especially for the family? Or had certain guests brought and bestowed pieces as hostess gifts?

Jodie easily pictured the finery, and how displaying and using it might have expressed hospitality to the cavalcade of distinguished guests known to have visited homes where one of the Wade Hamptons held court. After all, at one time the first Wade Hampton was one of the richest men in the nation, with swaths of property holdings in South Carolina and Mississippi.

The trail then went cold; there was no more contact with the Hampton descendant until Christmas season, when an exchange of annual cards and an occasional note began and kept the contact alive. Then one year the Fletchers noticed the Yuletide greeting was postmarked Sydney, Australia. The friend had moved to the metropolitan seaport to be nearer her mother and to begin graduate studies. She continued to reference the silver in every communiqué, and Jodie continued to offer her help if ever the silver was ready to come home.

Years elapsed. In all that time, Jodie often wondered what stories engraved in silver might be recounted by those pieces. But when the long-awaited letter finally arrived seven years after the chance encounter in Fiji, it was too late, at least for Jodie. Fletcher penned the sorrowful response that Jodie had died of an illness, but added that he would do whatever he could to honor the pledge made by his late wife. He, too, believed deep down the silver should be in South Carolina. Getting involved in the exchange Jodie had offered to ease years before would be a way of keeping her memory alive.

Now that the silver's owner was ready to follow her inclination to send her inherited silver back to South Carolina, she needed to determine a fair price for the family heirlooms. She found herself at an international disadvantage. In Australia, as in England, silver is identified and dated by a hallmark system dating to the 1300s, whereas in the United States only manufacturers' or makers' marks hold the key.

Convinced the silver's rightful place was in the Palmetto State, the South Carolina Archives and History Foundation stepped up and took the leading role in negotiating its repatriation. First, secure arrangements were made with the owner and Barbara, the Fletchers' friend. The silver was to be shipped to South Carolina where a professional antique silver appraiser was standing by in Columbia.

The carton crossed the Pacific Ocean; the contents then backtracked across the same continent it had traversed nearly a century earlier when Alfred Hampton went west to stake out a career. Appraiser Kay Durham spent much of the wait time revisiting the Hampton genealogy by studying Virginia Meynard's voluminous book entitled *The Venturers.*

When the much-anticipated carton finally arrived, foundation members opened the boxes in hushed awe. As each piece was unwrapped and examined, more questions were raised than answered.

The silver pieces had been handed down through seven generations, and had survived three wars, at least four fires, cross-country relocations, and ocean crossings. Lifted from cartons shipped from Australia were an ornate water pitcher, or ewer; gravy boats; a cream and sugar set; a single goblet; a sweetmeat dish; coin silver knives; and flatware bearing the single most distinguished initial in South Carolina: H.

Historians who had followed the story of the Hampton silver knew the line had paused with Alfred, the last of Wade Hampton III's four sons (two of whom were from his first marriage, and one of whom died in battle). Alfred had been born during the Civil War. His soldier father had been home to attend his birth in 1862, yet as the boy grew up, the two males often were separated by war, politics, and business.

In 1881, after Alfred earned his degree in civil engineering at the University of Virginia, he tried his hand at several kinds of work before staking his claim on a future out west. Wade Hampton III may well have counseled his youngest son to take Horace Greeley's advice, "Go West, young man, go West!"

The Library of Congress has on file a letter of introduction written by the father on his son's behalf. Did Alfred's famous father, involved with the most ambitious railroad project in South Carolina, foresee that railroads and surveying went hand in glove? Wade Hampton III already was serving on the board of the Charleston St. Louis Cincinnati.

But by the time President Grover Cleveland appointed Wade Hampton III the nation's first railroad commissioner in 1893, Alfred had been serving in the post of deputy county surveyor in El Paso, Texas, for a decade. There he met and, in 1895, married Frances Hermsen, who shared his love of horsemanship, a predilection of Hampton men.

Frances rode with Alfred as he surveyed the state of Sonora for the Mexican government. With no family of her own, the orphaned Hermsen undoubtedly had no dowry of family silver—the family silver had been part of Alfred's inheritance. As he prospered in his career, the couple's shared timeline appears to have been punctuated by the acquisition of new pieces of silver.

There was no provenance tucked into the carton from Australia, but there were still clues as to which family members had acquired which silver, and when. Monograms, the family crest, dates, and manufacturers' hallmarks provided part of the story, but much remained a mystery.

Were spoons and a tea strainer with ebony handles dated as early as 1890 once owned by one of the three Wade Hamptons, or did they mark the beginning of silver collected by Alfred and his wife? Flatware place settings included in the cache are from Gorham's New Castle pattern, not patented until 1895. They bear the mark of San Francisco jewelers Shreve and Sons. Were they wedding gifts to Alfred and Frances from new West Coast friends?

Alfred served in President Woodrow Wilson's cabinet as director of World War I war camps, and the couple did, for some of their years, live in the East, close to Baltimore's cultural artisans. Could that residency explain pieces hallmarked by world renowned Baltimore silversmiths?

But since much of Alfred's career involved immigration work, the couple spent many years in the West: Texas, Arizona, Montana, and California. How silver, so far removed from the nineteenth-century Southern culture, might have graced their tables is curious to imagine. But based on newer pieces' inclusion in the cache, silver continued to enter the Alfred Hamptons' lives well into the twentieth century. A bread and butter plate by Kirk was made sometime after 1902, a full century after the oldest piece that returned to South Carolina.

Could that oldest piece, a 1799–1800 sauce boat by London silversmiths Peter and Ann Bateman, have been a souvenir brought back by the first Wade Hampton from his 1821 travels to Europe?

More than a decade later, Wade Hampton III's descriptions of his own European sojourn sparked a courtship with his second wife, Mary Singleton McDuffie. Old Colonel Hampton personally recommended that Wade III help when Miss McDuffie needed advice about plantation business matters following her father's death. Was the patriarch match-making?

In contrast to her future husband, noted for his strong physique and demeanor, Mary was delicate and shy, with deep blue eyes and brown curls cascading to her shoulders. She preferred indoor activities to riding. The future couple's early conversations centered upon books and travel, and Wade Hampton's verbal travelogue of his European adventures so inspired Mary that she accompanied her aunt to the Continent in 1854. Four years later she ordered a trousseau from New York, and on January 27, 1858, the couple married. A single silver goblet in the Australian cache bears the bride's monogram, ending with the initials McD. Whether this piece was part of her family silver, an engagement gift, or even a wedding gift remains a mystery.

A large silver water pitcher crafted by Kirk in the French repousse style denoted style and status enjoyed by the family, at one time the richest in the country. Also in the repousse style—hammered from within to create a raised exterior pattern—was a gravy boat created around the mid-1800s. That the silver had survived, even when the family's fortunes were toppled through the spoils of war, by fire, or by economic reversals, made the collection an even greater treasure.

The earliest silver lifted from the boxes had ties to the Hampton-Preston House, now a house museum reflecting the family's contributions to state history. Between 1823 and 1873, South Carolina's most prominent family entertained local, national, and international dignitaries. Their homes—Millwood, Woodlands, and Diamond Hill—were veritable salons for political, social, cultural, and intellectual exchange.

Did John C. Calhoun carve roasted game with one of the coin silver knives? Was the repousse cream and sugar set passed to General Winfield Scott, and if so, did the sugar bowl contain crystals from the family's Louisiana plantation?

In May 1847 could spring strawberries have been served to Daniel Webster in the Kirk fruit basket? The outspoken senator from Massachusetts was in Columbia to visit his former senate colleague, William Preston. In 1845 following his congressional term, Preston returned home and became president of South Carolina College and served there until 1851. Webster, who had come to see first-hand the institution of slavery on a Southern plantation, was honored at a dinner party at the Hampton-Preston Mansion. The following day he toured another Hampton plantation, Millwood, and took the noon meal there. That evening, over dinner at the table of Dr. Robert Gibbes, Webster reiterated his position—that slavery was evil, but that the Constitution upheld it, and he upheld the Constitution. From what he'd seen that day, he said, "No change could be made which would benefit the slaves."

Wade Hampton III's public service, especially politics, made his home a haven for high-profile guests. So which piece might have been passed to Senator Henry Clay when he visited in 1847? A gravy boat, its handle graciously turned toward the Kentucky senator so he could grasp it with ease? On the evening Clay dined with the Hamptons, the sideboard likely displayed an imposing silver ewer.

When the silver shipment from Australia arrived, one very similar to that piece was unwrapped. The repousse piece with a horse's profile raised in relief clearly had been a riding trophy, one of many Wade Hampton won for his horsemanship. According to family legends, the first Wade Hampton had his little namesake grandson in a saddle at age four.

When French naturalist and ornithologist John James Audubon dined at the family table, he likely smiled at the exotic birds hand-painted on the Hampton family china set before him. The bone china dinner plates, encircled by a sherbet green border and the family crest, had been commissioned and shipped from England through the port of Charleston.

Jefferson Davis was a guest of the Hamptons on numerous occasions, but when he accepted Mary Boykin Chesnut's invitation for dinner, legend holds that Caroline Hampton Preston sent her cook over to help Mrs. Chesnut—and perhaps also sent the right silver for serving whatever the menu held in store for the evening.

How any Hampton silver survived what this family endured is part myth, part miracle. In February 1865 as Union troops marched toward Columbia with fire in their eyes, the Hampton women wrapped the family silver, china, and crystal in the heavy red damask taken down from Millwood's tall windows. From their gilded frames, family portraits and Troye horse paintings were removed, then all was packed in baggage wagons and conveyed by faithful servants to York, South Carolina.

There at the railroad stop, cousins awaited their frightened relatives. Left behind to be discovered and looted by Sherman's troops were Wade Hampton II's exquisite and valuable relic collection, statuary, and European paintings. Three Hampton homes were burned that night. The Hampton-Preston Mansion was spared because General John A. Logan fancied it for his headquarters.

Little more than a decade later, just as Wade Hampton III was preparing to attend a Confederate veterans' reunion in Charleston, arsonists leveled Millwood II, the only one of his three homes rebuilt after the Civil War. If the attendant legends can be believed, it was his bitterly contested 1876 gubernatorial election that was the motive for the fire. Household goods were lost, along with historic personal effects. How Confederate swords and family silver were saved is another mystery and another chapter in the family lore.

Of all the curiosity engendered by the repatriated silver, one of the most baffling questions was: Why now? Why, after all these years, was the distant Hampton heir willing to relinquish these long-held treasures? According to the story that had filtered back to South Carolina, the owner intended to use proceeds from the silver sale to set up a stipend for her son, whose mission work had inspired him to provide prostheses for deformed children in Africa.

Purchased by the South Carolina Archives and History Foundation through private donations, the Hampton silver is on long-term loan to the Historic Columbia Foundation. Some of the pieces are back in the same Hampton-Preston Mansion rooms they graced nearly 150 years ago. They whisper once more stories from a cataclysmic time. Their opulence speaks of lavish entertaining; their survival testifies to family tenacity.

CHAPTER SEVEN

South Carolina and Confederate Gold

Whenever there is gold, accounts are bound to be embellished. How it got to where it was, who knew of it, and when that knowledge was acquired all are part of the story. Glitter somehow illuminates the imagination. Many gold myths have "Happily Ever After" endings that explain where the gold is now.

But not when it comes to the Confederate gold.

Legends still abound that at least some of the treasury amassed to support the Confederacy is buried or hidden in South Carolina. Other states the treasure train passed through during its final maneuvers fan the flames of similar claims or rumors. Where the Confederate Cabinet traveled on its path from Richmond to the Deep South is well documented, but details are spotty when it comes to the gold that accompanied them.

Beginning that April day in 1865, in the chaos that ensued during their flight south, members of the Cabinet lost control of events and, along the way, the treasury dissipated—at least to some degree. Some of it was pulled straight off wagons to pay bedraggled soldiers slogging homeward, if indeed there was a home to return to. A little was paid for goods and services to feed the entourage in retreat.

Years earlier, secessionists had slipped diamond and pearl rings off their fingers, unpinned amethyst and opal brooches from lapels, and turned them over—along with other valuables, such as family silver—to the Confederate treasury. These contributions boosted morale, but often did not provide as much ready cash for the cause as the South's supporters might have imagined.

The war had been launched without benefit of a government treasury or even a sound financial policy. The Confederate treasury's nucleus—in the form of gold bullion—had been seized in the takeover of the U.S. Mint in New Orleans after Louisiana seceded from the Union in January 1861.

Funds were further bolstered when Georgia seceded in April and the U.S. Mint at Dahlonega was seized; its location was commandeered as the Confederacy's assay office for the duration of the war. When North Carolina seceded in May, contents of the U.S. Mint in Charlotte provided yet another jolt of financial stimulus, far more significant than the accumulated jewelry and silver donations.

How Confederate leaders miraculously fled Richmond with wagonloads of treasure in the midst of a frenzied evacuation left the escape's eyewitnesses shaking their heads. The treasurer and mastermind of the transition was a South Carolinian, and it is because of his involvement and leadership that this state is rumored to be a resting place for some of the riches.

Many tales have developed to explain what happened to the assets escorted to Richmond's rail depot that April evening. Strategy development and responsibility for the safe exit of the gold, silver, bonds, paper currency, and other notes, as well as valuables donated to the cause, fell to Confederate treasurer George Alfred Trenholm.

Trenholm ordered the valued cargo transferred by wagons to a railroad car bound for Danville, Virginia. Contents of banks in Richmond were heaped onto the conveyances as well. A second train was to transport an equally valuable cargo: a cadre of Richmond evacuees, ranging in rank and importance from Cabinet members themselves to army officers, treasury employees, and even very young midshipmen ordered to leave their ship, the *Patrick Henry*, on the James River to guard the transfer and see the treasury to its final destination, wherever that might be.

It had been late in the war that Trenholm was tapped to step into the Cabinet post held from February 21, 1861, to July 18, 1864, by fellow South Carolinian and friend, Christopher Gustavus Memminger. The German-born attorney and public servant resigned when he was worn down by criticism about the Confederacy's faltering economy, despite the fact that the Confederate Cabinet consistently failed to adopt his recommendations. Conversely, he disagreed with many of the Cabinet's proposed platforms.

Among the ironies of Memminger's three years' service was his stalwart fiscal belief in the gold dollar and his reluctant acquiescence to the issue of millions in paper money, depleting in value as the war raged on. Memminger would not support Secretary of State Judah Benjamin's proposal that the Confederate States of America (CSA) purchase and ship to England upwards of 100,000 bales of cotton in exchange for credits that could be applied to the acquisition of war hardware, even ships.

Another cotton-related wedge between the CSA and Great Britain came from the top. Rather than supply European demands for Southern cotton, Jefferson Davis believed creating a scarcity of the "White Gold" would force Britain and France to recognize the Confederate States.

Theorists have speculated that if cotton, in quantities upwards of 100,000 bales, had been shipped to Europe for credit early in the conflict, the South might have won the war. In the opening months, the Federal fleet still was widely dispersed; and, along the Southern Atlantic coastline, only three vessels capable of affecting a blockade were available. Those few ships had the daunting blockading responsibility for some 3,500 miles of coast.

Stepping into the treasury post at the eleventh hour was Trenholm, whose reputation as a master of diversion sprung from his corporate leadership as an importer and exporter. His successful tactics for running the Union's blockades radiated primarily out of Charleston's harbor, but also took in other international triangle trade involving England and Nassau, as well as Bermuda. Such business intelligence made his the most creative mind available to try outmaneuvering the Federals, especially as the Confederacy ran thin on options. Here's how his thinking had developed.

It had been Trenholm, a shipper's son, who at the age of sixteen joined an established Charleston shipping firm as an accountant, then worked his way into a partnership. He made a name for himself, in part, by authoring brazen articles opposing Northern tariff laws. His upward mobility also was boosted by his acquired knowledge of government jargon and procedures, especially concerning maritime matters.

Well in advance of the war, Trenholm anticipated how wartime would affect the import and export business. Just as it was emergent Southern leaders who began authorizing New York printers to issue the first Confederate currency months before a volley was fired, Fraser, Trenholm and Company began a five-ship line of trade between Charleston and Liverpool a full year prior to the firing on Fort Sumter.

From the hour of secession, declared in South Carolina on December 20, 1860, Charleston shipping businesses ceased complying with the egregious import tariffs set by Northern ports—as much as 50 percent of the value of the goods and commodities arriving on their wharves. When other Southern ports dropped their tariffs as well, Northern shipping concerns feared loss of business to their Southern competitors.

Trenholm's savvy agreement among the Confederate states, in which Southern cotton was conveyed across the Atlantic to Liverpool, generated proceeds that were banked in Britain. Profit margins allowed British agents to purchase provisions needed to fight the war. Brits in textiles were sympathetic to the Southern cause because they were dependent on cotton to keep their mills running in the black.

The goods—such as war materials and foodstuffs—represented a lifeline of Confederate supplies. Agile little ships delivered them clandestinely to Southern ports despite the efforts of Union blockades.

Trenholm's blockade-running ships, with official destinations in Nassau or Bermuda, often changed ships' paperwork or cargo before embarking upon the last five hundred miles or so to Charleston. To legitimize transactions, Fraser, Trenholm and Company established a Liverpool office; the Confederacy's head financial agent in Europe happened also to be headquartered there.

Trenholm was the South's banking liaison with European financial allies. His international business network positioned him to negotiate with shipping company principals at shipyards in both England and Scotland for the construction of vessels easily converted to naval warships. Britain's Foreign Enlistment Act mandated that ships could be built for foreign nations, but they could not be outfitted with battery. Armament often was added offshore, perhaps in Nassau, before the fast, little ships made the last leg of their journey.

Maritime ruses set up by this shrewd businessman involved sleights of hand concerning ships' names and ownerships, as well as manifests and even passengers in order to confuse the Union. Along with the Charleston port, which Trenholm knew like the back of his hand, other Southern ports received military hardware, foodstuffs, luxuries, and other scarce commodities. Items in short supply made it through the Federal blockades to be unloaded on wharves at Norfolk, Virginia; Beaufort, New Bern, and Wilmington, North Carolina; Savannah, Georgia; Pensacola, Florida; Mobile, Alabama; New Orleans, Louisiana; and Galveston, Texas.

Leaving these ports was as much "White Gold" as space on board would allow. On the occasions that fleeing blockade runners could not outpace pursuing Federal ships, enough cotton was heaved overboard to lighten the cargo load and regain the necessary competitive edge.

Such was the international commerce acumen and East Coast cunning of the man tapped by Confederate president Jefferson Davis to step into the post of treasurer. Many believe Trenholm could have turned the tide on the ailing economy—if only he had come to his post earlier.

But the Cabinet's heels were already dug in. They failed to approve Trenholm's suggestions; it was too late anyway. The Georgetown plantation owner joined the Cabinet ranks barely in time to be eligible for the scathing that would be attendant to his association once the bitter war ended.

How the Confederate treasury had in its possession at that late point in the fighting any war chest at all is mystery enough. Trenholm ordered sacks and tightly packed wooden crates bearing the Confederacy's official seal moved under dark tarpaulins. Inside were double eagle gold pieces, copper coins, and burgeoning crates of Mexican silver dollars that had paid for Southern cotton. There were nuggets, ingots, and bricks of both gold and silver.

The Confederacy's unofficial alliance with Great Britain accounted, to some degree, for the 18,000 pounds sterling of "Liverpool Acceptances," paper notes only negotiable in England. Priceless heirlooms, given by Confederate mothers, sisters, spinsters, and wives for the purchase of a warship, made the calculation even harder to place value on.

Also loaded onto those creaking wagons were deposits that cleaned out Richmond banks. From the time made until the time removed, these deposits always had been held separately from Confederate funds. Bonds and stacks of Confederate paper currency, their value leeching out of them with every hour that elapsed, were added into some accountings and evaluations and subtracted from others.

There are those who set the worth of that surreptitious cargo in the millions, but surely that would be a twenty-first century valuation. Those who rebuff such claims set the value far lower. Although the reputed worth of the treasury's remains varies from legend to legend, one consistently repeated figure is $500,000.

What and how much was in those wagonloads has been speculated over for more than a century and a half, and no one is any closer to a definitive answer now than then. One of the mysteries is how such a cargo got past Union scrutiny. Sure, bank deposits were carried out under the watchful supervision of Walter Philbrook, senior teller of the treasury department. And midshipmen, some as young as twelve years old, under the tutelage and orders of Captain William H. Parker, were guarding the transfer.

For this tentacle of the legend, there is more agreement than with other versions. Parker's young charges were among the last alive to continue telling their side of the story, and their versions included a stopover of a day or two in Danville, Virginia, before the closely guarded train headed on to Greensboro, North Carolina.

They had scarcely caught their collective breath when it became clear the entourage needed to move on, deeper south. As the train crossed the Dan River, the engineer was ordered to halt partway across the expanse, not once, but multiple times. Was some of the treasury released into the rushing water of the Dan River with hopes it could be retrieved at a safer time? The weight of low-value copper coins would have slowed the train's ascent up the next incline.

One development that has fueled this speculation for a century and a half is a patent application. William Lee Trenholm, son of Confederacy treasurer George Trenholm, sought

After leaving South Carolina, the Confederate treasury became harder to track.

and obtained U.S. Patent No. 269,139 for an underwater metal detector called a hypohydroscope. His description to the U.S. Patent Office alleged that the invention would enable its operator to "find objects at the bottom of streams." The notion conjures up images of searching or mining deep sections of the Dan River.

But the speculation withers with a look at the date of the patent: December 1882, nearly two full decades after the treasure train trudged across the trestle outside Danville, Virginia, just ahead of the Seventh South Carolina Cavalry guarding its flank.

Even before the 1876 death of his father, wealthy before, during, and after the war, William Trenholm was deeply involved in the family shipping business that entailed vessel maintenance, including submarine hulls. In his patent application, young Trenholm also stated the instrument would be used in the dredging and collecting of phosphate, an inexpensive plant fertilizer additive discovered in a unique geological strata of the Coastal Plain shortly after the war. Phosphate, a commodity in demand domestically as well as abroad, was a good business fit for Fraser, Trenholm and Company.

It is not known whether Trenholm the inventor ever tested his hypohydroscope in the Dan River. The father's vast holdings and obvious wealth held him above any suspicion that Confederate funds would have been commingled with his own. But his loyalty to the Confederacy might well have inspired him to secret the riches somewhere safe, bringing them out only after all danger had passed.

That is why one persistent legend suggests he may have buried treasure on one of his Georgetown plantations. Mentioned most often has been Annandale, deeded to his son-in-law, William Miles Hazzard, at year's end after the April surrender.

But at the time Trenholm was last in the company of the treasury, he was too ill to form strategy keen enough to divert such copious funds. South of Greensboro, the entourage was forced to disembark, transfer the freight to wagons again, and walk the remaining distance through spring mud. Federal troops had destroyed the railroad tracks. Miraculously, their clandestine maneuvers got the Cabinet to Charlotte, intended as another temporary capital.

Accompanied by his wife, Anna, the only female who had been part of the entourage, Trenholm entered Charlotte in an open horse-drawn ambulance. His sickbed was cosseted within the Tryon Street home of William Phifer, whose family risked much by harboring Confederates as they held, at the treasurer's bedside, what many scholars consider the Cabinet's last official meeting.

When he finally was able to leave Charlotte, he crossed into South Carolina before resigning as treasurer. The Trenholms spent a short time in Fort Mill as guests of the William White family. Then the couple made its way tediously to Abbeville, labeled the birthplace of the Confederacy because, a long five years earlier, tenets of secession had been hammered zealously there at a November 1860 meeting.

Trenholm, who only came onto the Cabinet in the war's waning months, had not been present at that fundamental meeting on what became known as Secession Hill. But it was there the couple was reunited with their daughters who had fled Richmond in advance of the Cabinet's evacuation. Trenholm already had limped on toward Columbia by the time the Cabinet arrived in Abbeville on May 2, 1865.

There in the parlor of his friend, Armistead Burt, President Davis listened soberly as his five brigade commanders—Ferguson, Dibrell, Vaughn, Duke, and Breckenridge—convinced their leader that resources were exhausted and that only further misery would result from fighting on. It was then that Jefferson uttered "All indeed is lost."

Nevertheless, a few Confederate leaders still held out hope that the treasury trove, wherever it was, might be the underpinnings of eventual victory. Interestingly, sixteen years later, the publication of *The Rise and Fall of the Confederate Government*—a two-volume opus by none other than the former Confederate president Jefferson Davis—led to a flurry of articles and books all pledging to telling the true story of what happened to the Confederate gold. But despite all the stories and all the sustained efforts to find the treasure, the mystery remains unsolved.

CHAPTER EIGHT

Mars Bluff's Atomic Bomb

Boredom and restlessness aren't all bad. Back in the spring of 1958, they saved the lives of three Florence County children. If games in their backyard playhouse had not become tiresome on a certain March afternoon, the little girls would not have meandered to their side yard. Fortunately, they did; otherwise, they might easily have been the first Americans obliterated on native soil by a nuclear bomb.

On the front porch of a traditional farmhouse, Effie Gregg was sewing as her two daughters—Frances and Helen—played with their cousin. One of the county's most stylish women, Mrs. Gregg was known for her talent with fabric and needle. She made her own dresses and the girls', too.

In the shed Frances and Helen's father Walter Gregg and uncle Bill Gregg were tinkering with a farm implement when—without warning—something fell from the sky, cratered into their yard, and blasted to smithereens their farm site set back in a clearing in the unincorporated community of Mars Bluff near Florence, South Carolina.

The explosion blasted out the farmhouse windows, peeled off asbestos sheathing, and splintered wood. Trees near the house snapped like twigs, and dirt clouded the wreckage. On US 301, several miles from the impact, the boom from the explosion turned a motorist's car completely around in the road. Closer to the Gregg's former home, Mount Mizpah Baptist Church was partially destroyed.

With no idea what had just happened, the Greggs' first concerns were medical. At the local hospital doctors examined cuts Effie Gregg suffered to her head, and Bill Gregg to his back.

Frances and Helen's little cousin, Ella Davies, who had been visiting that afternoon, was the only one in the family whose injuries required an overnight stay in the Florence hospital. It was while he was waiting for the last suture to be tied off in his little niece's face that Walter Gregg learned from authorities, who caught up with him there, just what had befallen his homestead.

The blast had been caused by an atomic bomb that had fallen out of an accidentally opened bomb bay in the belly of an Air Force B-47E. Gregg knew little more at that time. However, as the patriarch learned what had brought about the explosion, there were new concerns. Was radioactivity an additional horror to consider? It was the Cold War era, and, to most Americans, the A-bomb meant radiation, and radiation was a death sentence.

Fearful that even their clothing might have been contaminated by nuclear fallout, the Greggs faced the ominous truth: They had been lucky to get out with their teeth and their hair. Even the clothes on their backs had to be stripped for examination; could they be contaminated?

The ruined rural site was quickly cordoned off by authorities, both military and civil, so the Greggs could not return to the wreckage that had once been their home. The good news, they were told, was that the thirty-kiloton bomb did not contain its removable core of fissionable uranium and plutonium, only conventional explosives.

An atomic bomb, dropped accidentally over Mars Bluff,
South Carolina, in 1958, created a deep crater that continues to
remind area residents of the incident.

On the scene in record time, photographer Tom Kirkland of the *Florence Morning News* gave the gears of his Speed Graphic camera a workout. Thinking he was finished for the day, Kirkland had been heading to his parked car, when, by a stroke of luck, a friend wheeled up and said, "Get in." A couple of objections didn't work, so finally Kirkland got in. His friend, a Civil Air Patrol major—wearing his dress uniform which bore a striking resemblance to an Air Force major's uniform—filled Kirkland in on the way to the bomb site. Richard Ward had heard about the explosion from another friend who had been listening in on a Federal Aviation Administration radio frequency. What the friend heard was a navigator bombardier's expletives that accompanied his exclamation: "I dropped it!"

Ward wheeled up to the dirt road leading to the Gregg's property in a cloud of dust. When he told local officials blocking the way he was there to secure the area until the Air Force representatives arrived, the major was waved right on through. The site was eerily absent of any humans, military or civilian, when Kirkland and Ward closed their car doors softly, feeling they were encroaching upon something otherworldly. The seasoned photographer, a World War II veteran, photographed frame after frame of what had been, until just minutes earlier, the family home of a railroad man who farmed soybeans and raised pigs part-time.

Ward wanted to stick around, but as soon as Kirkland got what he needed, he hitched a ride back into town and hurried to the newspaper's darkroom to develop the pictures, not knowing yet whether he—or his film—had been exposed to radiation.

Impatient, he jiggled the processing paper in his developing trays with tongs, hoping what floated to the top would not be fogged. Kirkland wiped his beaded brow on his shirt sleeve and breathed a sign of relief when solid images surfaced. Then, fortunately for history, he had the presence of mind, and the military savvy, to secure his negatives in a very safe place.

When he finally got home that night, his phone rang three times. Three wire services asked him if he could get them aerial shots of the site as soon as possible; three times he said yes.

That night a little neighbor boy of the Greggs admitted to his father he had disobeyed family rules: He had left his own yard and gone over to see what all the commotion at the Greggs' was about. He was picking up debris off the ground, probably pieces of bomb casings, putting them in his pocket, when a sheriff's deputy clapped him on the shoulder and told him the stuff was probably radioactive.

In what the little boy feared would be one of his last conversations with his dad, he said tearfully he wouldn't be milking the cow that night. He was probably going to vaporize at any moment. This was probably it. He had disobeyed, and now he was going to pay the price.

The following day, as the Gregg family collected themselves in a local hotel, having no idea yet how long their stay would be, people around town were reading the first accounts in the daily paper, poring over Kirkland's pictures.

Kirkland, meanwhile, had made his way to the airport where, less than twenty-four hours earlier, the first report of trouble had been received on the two-way radio. He counted on a friend who often took him up to make aerial photographs, but the friend's plane was grounded for its annual inspection.

Dejected that he would have to renege on assignments of a lifetime from three major wire services, Kirkland shifted camera bags on his shoulder and was heading back to his car when a different friend swung into the parking lot. Through his rolled down window, he told Kirkland he was going to fly up for a look at the crater. Did Kirkland want to come along? Did he?

In the air, the single engine Cessna 170 was able to position Kirkland plenty close enough over the former Gregg homestead. Kirkland bracketed roll after roll of four by five film, shooting with the speed he usually reserved for the occasional NASCAR crash scenes at the nearby Darlington Race Track. In the short time the recreational pilot had the photographer in the air, Kirkland was able to squeeze off a variety of shots dissimilar enough to satisfy each of the three news services. When the Cessna shuddered to a stop at the Florence County Airport, the first half of Kirkland's task had been accomplished.

The photographer hurried back to the newspaper's darkroom, canned his film, and stirred the developing trays. As quickly as his aerial photographs of the crater and surrounding damage dried, they were snapped up by the three news services and put out on the wires to begin telling the world about the colossal accidental bombing.

According to the story that has been perpetuated for more than half a century, the pebble that initiated the bizarre ripple effect can be traced back to a Cold War training mission.

The saga began just two hundred miles away near Savannah, Georgia, at Hunter Air Force Base. Hub of strategic bomber activity, Hunter AFB was home to the famed 2nd Bomber Group, the oldest continuously operating bomber group in the nation's military aviation history. The unit had been created in 1918 to serve in France under General Billy Mitchell.

On the day in question, a 308th Bombardment Wing crew comprised of three captains—Earl Koehler, pilot; Charles Woodruff, co-pilot; and Bruce Kulka, navigator bombardier— hastened to get off the ground and into the air.

The practice bomb run, code named Operation Snow Flurry, from Georgia to Bruntingthorpe Air Base, England, was part of the Unit Simulated Combat Mission and Special (or Nuclear) Weapons Exercise. The maneuver was to include a midair refueling drill off Canada's east coast in addition to a practice run over England.

Along with the plane piloted by Koehler, three other aircraft were competing to see which crew signaled the ground first indicating "Mission Accomplished." Computers would calculate the accuracy of the pseudo-bombing. At stake (well before they learned a family's safety and home would weigh in) were points for the prevailing team. In advance of the important mission launch, not one but two generals arrived on site for the briefing, throwing the full heft of their rank behind their emphasis.

It had taken a crew of two specialists more than an hour to wrestle the bomb into its harness, yet they still experienced problems setting the steel locking pin into place. Finally, the duo called over a weapons release systems supervisor with far more experience. He ordered the bomb manually lifted up so the pin could be set in place. Use of a hammer was required to seat the pin.

Taking care of this issue had eaten time off the crew's clock and its original estimated time of departure. The training crew knew they would take off with negative points if they didn't get the plane in the air by 10:30 a.m.

During that period in the nation's military history, it was policy that the pin be released before takeoff, then, once the aircraft attained altitude of five thousand feet, the pin was to be re-set until drop time. Years later, declassified documents confirmed the release mechanism for the steel pin was not checked again before takeoff.

Only part one of the training maneuver went without a hitch. The pin was released successfully as the plane took off. When the pilot's altimeter confirmed he was flying at the appropriate altitude, he pulled the lever that, according to training and protocol, would re-set the pin.

It didn't. Again and again he tried in vain, but the indicator kept telling him the pin was not set properly.

So the pilot ordered the navigator-bombardier to go back into the bomb bay to assess and fix the problem. While Kulka was getting himself prepared to insinuate his taut, concise frame into the very tight area, already accommodating a 7,600-pound bomb called Fat Boy for good reason, the pilot depressurized the entire plane and all three crewmen went on oxygen.

Kulka had to slip out of his parachute harness—there was no way to fit into the bomb bay with it on—and he was holding onto his oxygen cylinder manually as he slithered into position and began feeling his way, bare-fingered, to the top of the bomb where the pin was located. He was hoping to find out what was interfering with the pin's positioning.

His short arms were no match for the huge curvature of the bomb. He hugged and pawed at its exterior helplessly, its slickness thwarting his attempts to jockey himself around it. His rodeolike maneuvers resembled pig riding. Ironically, "Pig" was the nickname Air Force flyboys had given to such bombs because of their unwieldy size.

With all his might, Kulka believed that if he could just get to the nose and look at the harness, he could see immediately what was wrong. Just for a moment, he thought he'd hit pay dirt when his bare stumpy fingers, cold at 15,000 feet, latched onto something cylindrical. Surely it was the pin. He tried to get a grip on it.

Suddenly, the cold metal "pig" shifted, metal clinked on metal, and the bomb pressed against the bomb bay door—with Kulka still astride it. The 7,700 pounds of bomb and airman pressed the bay open, first an inch, then Kulka could feel it wanting to give another inch. A draft of spring air rushed through the opening.

Kulka scrambled, shimmied, and, with white knuckles, hung on for dear life as the bomb bay doors opened further. Gravity prevailed.

With a gulp, the bomb was sucked out into the atmosphere above the Greggs' farm and fell 15,000 feet through wispy cirrus clouds toward the terra firma plowed thoughtfully by Gregg before he planted his soybeans.

Grabbing hold of anything solid he could grasp, Kulka clamored back into the belly of the plane. When his heart left his throat and settled back into his chest, he thought back over every move he had made. Could he have grabbed the emergency-release lever and not the pin?

He did not have to tell the pilot the bomb had released. The Stratojet lurched as it was accidentally relieved of its payload. What cratered into the Mars Bluff farmland was a Mark 6 thirty-kiloton bomb.

According to regulations, the pilot was to report immediately to base in the event of an accidental drop. In training, the special code name had been emphasized, but it had never been uttered, so when the pilot called it in, personnel at Hunter AFB did not recognize Broken Arrow. No one responded to the radioed transmission.

How else could the pilot alert his superiors to what had just happened? After trying every other alternative he could think of, Koehler radioed the tower at the Florence County Airport and prevailed upon the operators there, through an open, uncoded message, to relay to the air base that Aircraft 35-1876A had lost a device.

A civilian pilot cleared to land at the Florence airport picked up the open message, and out leaked the word.

From the air, the Florence response personnel on the ground looked like ants beginning to make a line out to the Gregg place. The flight crew was in a high altitude no-man's land. They waited for instructions and finally were told what they realistically expected but dreaded to hear: abort the mission, the game was over. But they could not land, not back at Hunter AFB, not anywhere, not for hours. They had too much fuel in their tanks. One accident for March 11, 1958, was enough. So they had to fly around until they finally had burned off enough fuel, then land where they had started such a short time earlier, full of confidence they would win the weapons exercise.

Compared with the several tries it took for the flight crew to communicate its problem to headquarters, it didn't take long for Air Force brass to storm Florence. Confirming only that "an incident occurred," they were more concerned with shutting down the news that already had circled the globe. One of their first stops was the office of the *Florence Morning News.* At the door of the darkroom, they demanded Kirkland's pictures. The photographer handed over what had already run in that day's paper.

The brass explained one reason they wanted to quiet the crowds was out of public concern that there might be radioactive material at the site. Kirkland said they need not check; if his film had turned black, they would have cause to worry, but his pictures came out just fine.

Not only did the U.S. government blast a hole in the Greggs' property with a detonator device equal to about six thousand pounds of TNT, but they significantly undervalued the family's property. The Greggs had very little money to start their lives over.

Meanwhile, the Air Force continued checking the grounds with Geiger counters, but never a bleep was registered. Treasure hunters still skulk around the property, hoping for souvenirs. Parts of the bomb casing were found as far as seven hundred yards from the crater, and some parts still are missing.

More than fifty years after the accident forever altered a farm family's life—as well as a few U.S. Air Force policies—mysterious events that suggest government interference continue to occur. For instance, when a Gregg family member put a few souvenir fragments up for sale on eBay, they were pulled from the site before anyone placed a bid.

And today locals still refer to the bomb's unexpected arrival as "the incident over at Mars Bluff."

CHAPTER NINE

Civil War Graffiti

Paper was scarce during the Civil War, but soldiers—fearing they might never make it home, never get to tell their stories—used other surfaces on which to leave history evidence of their existence. Claiming homes and other buildings as spoils of war, they scratched their names, and sometimes those of their regiments, on walls. There, in rooms where families had gathered joyfully until the war between North and South interrupted their lives, soldiers had their say for posterity.

In an inland church, an explanation was penciled onto a wall, just above a doorjamb. In a coastal plantation's dank basement, so low a man had to stoop to enter, Union soldiers left on the wall some sentiment, their names, sometimes rank and attachment, which also revealed where they hailed from.

They may not have known it then, but their graffiti was as much a practice of soldiering as fighting itself. Historical references to graffiti can be found dating as early as the times in which the Greeks set sail for Troy. Like the mythological

Achaeans, real soldiers throughout the ages have verified their own mythology by leaving behind marks to represent themselves and their feelings about the time and conflict in which history had placed them.

In South Carolina, even before history was being formally recorded, petroglyphs were scratched onto a rock outcrop in what is now Pickens County. Perhaps this was an early form of graffiti. The writing on that wall meets at least this criterion: The markings were left behind for discoverers to muse over the meanings.

Military graffiti inscriptions appear to convey not only the mentality of the young soldier, but also his raw and intimate emotions, his keen sense of immediacy. The scribblings and scrawlings have been left behind for future inhabitants and visitors to interpret from their own perspectives.

When the tide of soldiers ebbed after the American Civil War, they left behind many tangible reminders of the grim conflict. As afterthoughts, old marble monuments were erected and carved with names and dates. Brass buckles, buttons, and shards of swords are still found today by field and hobby archaeologists.

But some of the most haunting are marks left by random soldiers, ripped from their ranks by wounds that had them faltering on their march. Was it their poignant sense of passing through, never to return to that locale again, that compelled them to verify their presence by marking on walls of plantation homes, public buildings, even places of worship?

Just whose sentiments were expressed a century and a half ago? Was the day they made their marks on the wall a turning point in their lives? Did they make it home post-war to forge a family? A future?

From fatalistic to satirical, markings convey whatever feelings the soldiers were experiencing at the time. Was a certain cavalryman leaving his last will and testament? Was this artilleryman poking fun at follies of the time—including politicians and high-ranking officers? Loneliness, angst, and, as poet John Keats penned, ". . . fears that I shall cease to be" were conveyed by personally emblematic markings left to befuddle and bewilder posterity.

Boredom may have moved the hands that penned graffiti at sites such as Cassina Point and Seabrook House, both on Edisto Island. Tramping across wide-plank floors stretching throughout the airy two-and-one-half story, marsh-side plantation home called Cassina Point, Union soldiers left more than boot marks. From the basement's dirt floor rose walls used like blackboards by enlisted men billeted there.

In that raised brick basement, young New Hampshire soldiers scraped into plaster shapes of ships from their nautical bearings, or perhaps ships on which they had trained. Mysterious vertical sets of numerals, resembling formulas, can still be seen today along one of the doorjambs.

Members of the Third New Hampshire Infantry squiggled finely detailed vessels, practiced their languishing math, and outlined lovers' names. But were the ships whose pale shapes remain visible to this day those on which the New Englanders had sailed into the Charleston Harbor—or ships of dreams? Could the numerals left behind the doorjamb have been military codes? Were the faraway lovers' affections requited?

Lower Russell Creek's marsh still separates that plantation home from another, even finer one that Union officers occupied. Seabrook House, a two-and-a-half story, Early Republic–style, wood-framed cotton plantation home set at Steamboat Landing, was built in 1810. Its founder also operated a ferry from there, but the owners in residence complied when General Lee gave evacuation orders. Federal troops had their pick of the empty homes, and they chose the very best. Handwriting on the wall in the open, airy house occupied for staff headquarters allows for a close comparison between officers' graffiti and that scrawled by enlisted men, just across the marsh at Cassina Point. Whether the officer's penmanship reveals differences in training and background is debatable; it appears soldiers far from home feel the same emotions.

In the Marlboro County Court House, ribald comments were left behind in the index of a book ripped from a shelf. The author left those unrepeatable comments anonymously, but he did leave a note in the front of the volume referencing Shawneetown and Equality, both listed on Gallatin County, Illinois, maps. The author of this graffiti did not date his entry, but that mystery is easy to solve. On March 7, 1865, Union troops from the 17th Army Corps of Sherman's army swarmed into Bennettsville.

Perhaps some soldiers picked up pen, chalk, or the projectile end of a bullet and made their marks just because their colleagues were up to the mischief. That would explain why some graffiti locations are nearly covered in it.

Regret, maybe even remorse, is the apparent emotion penned in an apology on the wall of the Old Brick Church in Winnsboro. One of few eighteenth-century meeting houses remaining in the state, the small, rectangular structure built in 1788 is simple and unadorned with a gable roof and unornamented windows. Its floorboards and pews were of locally hewn wood. After Reverend James Rogers organized the Associate Reformed Synod of Carolinas there in early May 1803, the church membership grew in numbers until the Civil War broke out, and then males joined the Confederate army en masse.

The graffiti apology, penciled on the wall, concerned the damage done to the church by Union troops. On orders, they had removed part of the flooring and woodwork to rebuild a bridge across Little River. "Citizens of this community: Please excuse us for defacing your house of worship, so much. It was absolutely necessary to effect a crossing over the creek, the Rebs had destroyed the bridge. A Yankee."

Some time after the war, the building was repaired; the graffiti has been kept legible for future generations to ponder the plaintive message. The little church remained in active use until 1920, and now is open only for annual commemorative services.

The contrast between the ribald comments left in Bennettsville and the benevolent apology found in Winnsboro shows soldiers' varying reactions to being caught in the crosshairs of war. These and other marks are indelible links to America's most trying hour: countrymen in a battle of wills.

Besides their purely verbal messages, the markings raise questions in other ways. Were drawings of quality indicative of some art training? Did the penmanship indicate a level of educational attainment? Did the size of the graffiti divulge ego? Or just bravado? Did markings nearly ceiling high indicate they had been made by a very tall soldier, and conversely, were low markings left by soldiers short of stature? Or by patients lying horizontally on cots?

McLeod Plantation on James Island has been violated by various military occupations throughout its centuries. A drawing of a hand with a finger pointing to the adjutant's makeshift office does not reveal the home army of its author: British, Confederate, or Union? The main house at McLeod Plantation served as headquarters for General States Rights Gist's Brigade, as well as Confederate unit headquarters, a commissary, and a field hospital until the island fell to the invading Federal army in the spring of 1865.

When Confederate forces evacuated Charleston on February 17, 1865, Federal troops took over the property and continued to use the plantation as both a field hospital and officers' quarters. The front parlor was used as a surgical theater. Outside, soldiers of the first official black units in the United States armed forces, the 54th and 55th Massachusetts, were encamped at the site.

But might the graffiti found there in the main house represent an earlier occupation—by Confederates? Or an even earlier war? The plantation, first shown on a 1695 map, was reputedly a vibrant place during the colonial period. The plantation was part of Sir Henry Clinton's encampment; the British general created his strategy for the Siege of Charleston at the site.

Nearby, at Secessionville Manor, signatures left by Confederate soldiers on walls of the first floor hallway have been preserved and framed by the home's twenty-first-century owners. In all these years, the markings have not been painted over. Remarkably, all who have lived there recognized the indelible history the graffiti represents.

A century and a half after the Civil War, construction workers undertaking the restoration of the historic Lancaster County Courthouse scraped away a mottled layer of paint and found beneath it a haunting face. The portrait had been

PHOTO BY GINGER R. MUNNERLYN

Someone, probably a Union soldier held against his will in Lancaster, passed his time by drawing poignant images on the courthouse walls.

left there sometime during the war era by someone unhappy at being confined there, someone who would rather have been elsewhere.

The graffiti that reveals itself again in this century varies in styles of drawing and handwriting. One would-be portraitist, whose profile of an unidentified subject exhibits latent talent, perhaps benefited from some schooling in the arts before he took up arms to help preserve the Union. Now he was in prison, using the walls as his canvas.

So, as the condition of the nineteenth-century courthouse required twenty-first century restoration, local historians began delving again into the public building's background. They, along with city and county officials, are hoping to piece together how, by whom, and when the graffiti might have been drawn on the ground floor walls of the courthouse. Designed by South Carolina native Robert Mills, who also designed the Washington Monument, the courthouse featured Tuscan columns, windows and doors set in recessed arches, and free air circulation on the lower (jail) level, quite unusual for the time. One would think prisoners being held in such handsome accommodations would be respectful enough not to write on the walls, but apparently they were unmoved by Mills's design.

Among the greatest mysteries attendant to the graffiti are two: Why did some owners protect the writings for posterity, and how much of it are we missing? You would think many owners finally able to return to their beloved homes would want to rid themselves of any reminders of the Great Unpleasantness, as some still call the American Civil War. Those whose sense of history prevailed and inspired them to protect the markings, by not painting or wallpapering over them, have continued the sacrifice they made a century and a half ago by evacuating their property when ordered to do so. Leaving the markings intact affects the use and décor of the spaces in which soldiers expressed themselves so freely.

For some, the marks have added character, even persona to their dwellings. But they are sober reminders, nevertheless. At Secessionville Manor on James Island, some of the names inscribed in the center hall appear to have been retraced in pencil—more than once—perhaps altering the appearances of the names. Someone, after the soldiers retreated, wanted to be sure the signatures remained legible.

At the Miles Brewton House in Charleston's historic district, family members owning the property have added to the example of graffiti left behind by Sir Henry Clinton when he occupied the distinctive home, using it as his headquarters. When America won its independence, the general retreated to England. On the same under-mantel where Clinton left his autograph and an anonymous graffitist sketched a bust, subsequent family members have penned their own signatures.

But much more graffiti has vanished than is visible today. When ailing Confederacy treasurer George Trenholm got to Columbia after his circuitous sojourn from Richmond, Virginia, he found his home burned. Scrawled behind the door of the only remaining room were signatures of five Federal soldiers who took credit for the arson.

In the early 1920s, Clyde Bresee visited the abandoned Vanderhost plantation house on Kiawah Island. In neat, open script he found: "The 55th Massachusetts Volunteers. How are you, General Beauregard? Veritas vincit ('the truth conquers.')."

Although the Lancaster Courthouse is making its graffiti accessible, little other graffiti remains in places the public can see it, although occasionally homes bearing Civil War graffiti are included on seasonal tours. Reproductions of the markings have made their way into books, manuscripts, and reports, ensuring that the soldiers' original intention be fulfilled—that their presence in a certain place on a certain historic day be recorded for history.

CHAPTER TEN

Hoofprints through History

For more than five centuries, their ripple effect has radiated quietly through the New World. But on what beaches did marsh tackies first leave hoofprints? How did horses from a noble Spanish equestrian bloodline end up being called common? And how have the distinctive equines gently and surely insinuated themselves into the state's culture?

They are simultaneously artifact and a contemporary piece of living history, and now the marsh tacky has been named the State Heritage Horse of South Carolina. In their blood is definitive confirmation they have outlasted conquerors, colonists, tribes, and enemies. Their arrival in the New World created quite a splash.

Actually, their Atlantic foray may have been more of a series of splashes and broad, saltwater belly busts. DNA testing affirms that the marsh tackies are of Spanish stock, and one theory suggests they were en route to the New World in Spanish ships when a squall broke the vessels apart. Horses tethered in primitive hammocks of leather and rope for a full season at sea broke free of their shackles and were liberated.

A more likely scenario, however, is that they were pushed overboard. The Spaniards had no other way to get the horses off the creaky wooden ships on whose decks they had been confined all those months. Lancers were counting on the steeds to take them into a new continent's wilderness.

The horses swam naturally to pale-sand jetties, islands, or beaches and shook off the effects of their tumultuous journey. Then, after foraging on high sea grass and nibbling a few bay berries, they began serving mankind in all the ways they could.

The marsh tackies' purity, owed to their relative isolation on the state's islands and coasts, makes them valuable genealogical evidence of a bloodline that, in Spain, diluted over centuries of inbreeding.

Small of stature, the equines may have arrived as "drop offs" on the coast of what later would become known as South Carolina. If their first forays on this continent did not result from being jettisoned by Spanish explorers, they may have been part of stock brought over a century later by Spanish settlers.

Although conventional wisdom has supported the supposition that marsh tackies descended from Andalusian steeds of Spanish conquistadors, other tales of their origins have been made plausible by punctuating legends with certain well-placed facts.

Only with Christopher Columbus's arrival did domestic horses take their natural places in this hemisphere. Both horses and donkeys were on board that second voyage in 1493, and, contrary to Spain's cultural policies that men ride only stallions, Columbus persuaded King Ferdinand to include mares for the expedition. Carefully selected for this important, history-making role, the mares were to be ridden, and also serve as breeding stock. Reigning over the finest horses in the world, the Spanish king and queen recognized the importance of establishing a viable breeding herd. So why were some of the first horses to leave hoof marks on the New World not among Spain's best?

One legend that has persisted for more than five centuries seems quite plausible, in light of horsemen embarking on a journey of such uncertainty. On the night before the seventeen ships set sail on Columbus's second exposition, some of the lancers sold their fine royal-issued steeds and, with the monetary differential, bought rounds of drinks for their friends and families, whom they feared they would never see again. In place of the steeds that would have assured Spain's New World prominence as superlative horse breeders, the lancers swapped for nags of questionable quality.

As early as the Middle Ages, the Spaniards were associated with horsemanship. The small but powerful nation was famous around the known world for its riding and breeding acumen. Because of the weight of armor worn and weapons carried by knights, horses were bred to distribute the weight.

Centuries before Columbus launched his second voyage on October 13, 1493, bringing with him horses as well as other livestock for introduction into the New World, the Spanish had taken note of fast little desert horses ridden by invading Moors. These smaller horses, ridden with short stirrups, allowing the Moors to stand up and throw their lances while advancing, gave the Spaniards a tutorial on breeding horses for battle mobility.

During the ensuing 780 years in which the Moors continued to invade Spain, Spaniards cross-bred the quick little Moorish Barbs, as they were known, with their own steeds. The resulting horse was faster, more agile. Such breeding made for a more tenacious animal, and for those selected for the expedition to the New World, that trait was essential for the perpetuation of the stock.

Conditions for transporting horses in ships of the day were gruesome at best. First, the "chosen" horse was fitted into a sling; next the animal was hoisted onto the ship by means of pulleys. Every inch of space aboard ship was as precious as the cargo the expedition's leader expected to return with. Although Spaniards characteristically were closely bonded with their steeds, that relationship unfortunately did not earn the unsuspecting horses any better portage.

For one thing, space allocated for them on the small deck was as minimal as possible. In all fairness to the Spaniards, their methods of transport had the safety of the horses at heart. They swung them in a hammocklike suspension system secured to the ship's structure by rings and ropes to make sure the horses did not slide overboard. To prevent holes being kicked in the deck, the Spaniards tied the horses' front legs together. Because there was no realistic estimated time of arrival, the horses' food and water was rationed from a tiny manger attached in front of the suspension system.

Exposure to naturally cruel elements—salt water and searing sun—surely thrust these horses abruptly into adaptation. They were packed like sardines onto a tiny deck without enough to eat or drink. Survival of the fittest began on the high seas. Records show between 25 and 50 percent of the horses expired before the ships made landfall.

Those who made it across the Ocean Sea, as it was called in those days, left the first hoofprints on the New World's beaches. Their imprints provided early proof they could make it in a harsh environment. Once land was sighted, horses that had been confined for months were unshackled and pushed overboard to swim to shore. There was no other way to get them to solid ground.

The Spanish occupied the Port Royal Sound area in 1521, a century before the English colony of Jamestown, Virginia. They returned in 1566 and founded the colony of Santa Elena and Fort San Marcos on Parris Island. Somewhere along the timeline of Spanish presence in the New World, these horses created their own identity.

Brought to bear riders who would thrash through wilderness, claiming riches and espousing Christianity, enough of these horses eluded the conquistadors, then later the settlers, to splinter off. Called feral, sometimes near-feral, they defaulted to their instincts and survived.

But there are other theories. Some years ago a naturalist living, researching, and writing in the Lowcountry hypothesized that the horse actually was a mixture of Seminole and Chickasaw horses that had been crossed with English thoroughbreds. That theory leaves years of the tackies' history unaccounted for.

Some scholars speculate that Native Americans rounded up some horses wandering loose around St. Augustine, Florida, and led them, as pack animals, along deerskin trade routes to Charleston. Also, a journalist researching and writing in the Lowcountry during the mid-1970s tracked their presence and wrote that horses matching the tackies' description were introduced to the Southwest in 1755.

The horses' surefootedness and agility in the bottomlands gave some of their most famous riders a competitive edge against the Redcoats as early as the Revolutionary War. Gen. Francis Marion's "Irregulars" arrived to champion freedom's cause on their own mounts, often marsh tackies. That his troops were mounted on horses from their own farms, superbly adapted to the region's rugged, swampy topography, was an incidental technical advantage exploited by the "Father of American Guerrilla Warfare." When British lieutenant colonel Banastre Tarleton realized the marsh tacky was one of Marion's secret weapons, he seized one for himself. He was riding it when his troops took Charleston. The smaller equines

Marsh tackies break out of the pines, proving their proficiency at negotiating South Carolina backwoods.

"requisitioned" from locals replaced English horses that had been lost in a sea storm.

It was Tarleton who gave Marion his nickname, the Swamp Fox, and Brits also added the noun "tacky" to the adjective "marsh" in applying a name that quite obviously has stuck. In that Anglo-Saxon definition, tacky means "common" or "cheap," and while it is true that, for many years, the horses seemed always available and plentiful in South Carolina's Low-country, they also had made themselves indispensable by that time in their history.

During the Civil War marsh tackies served the Confederate cavalry which, unlike Northern troops who were issued mounts, were expected to provide their own horses. The precedent had been set by their ancestors as they fought for independence from England. Riding familiar horses turned out to be an early advantage to Southern forces.

The horses' military service continued as many of them served in the Coast Guard's Mounted Beach Patrol during World War II, protecting the beaches, and therefore the mainland, from enemy spies and saboteurs in submarines.

When the automobile took over American culture, tackies quietly faded into history's background. By that time these formerly spirited creatures were described by scientists as "calm and level-headed."

Over the years, they survived—sometimes barely—by their own wit and instincts. Foraging for themselves in relative isolation on barrier islands, just far enough out in the channels to be inconvenient to herd up, they were left pretty much alone. Just as Spain audaciously claimed the New World, anyone who could catch one—and they were easy to catch—could claim a marsh tacky, and with it, responsibility for its care. Often owners were local farmers within Gullah communities where the Sea Island culture mirrored some of the small horses' scrappy heritage.

Occasionally herds flourishing on barrier islands with little human presence would be rounded up by farmers or hunters to fulfill work or domestic needs for horses. More recently, modern man recognized once again the plucky horses' positive qualities and characteristics, and began protection and breeding measures to guard against their extinction. By then, their numbers had diminished to an estimated two hundred purebred marsh tackies.

The early 1950s marked a turning point in their survival. It was then that one D. P. Lowder began investing his Saturday afternoons in short drives over to Hilton Head. There he would pick up one or two just wandering the untamed island and bring them home, just as his father had brought home the tackies Lowder rode as a Lowcountry child.

But that was before real estate developer Charles Fraser's vision of Hilton Head as a resort destination was realized. Bridges and vehicles to cross them diminished the importance of marsh tackies that, in relatively modern times, had transported children to school and waited, untethered, in the schoolyard until the dismissal bell rang.

Through the week tackies had pulled plows through garden soil that produced tomatoes, beans, squash, melons, even a little remaining sea island cotton. Brushed down and bearing different tack, they had been Sunday's ride to church.

Although taken for granted, like wild sea oats swaying on sandy embankments or Spanish moss cascading from live oak trees, marsh tackies became fixtures in the state's history. Their innate ability to wrest themselves from swamp mud by easing onto one side until their footing could be recovered gave them a solid reputation as the horse to have in the swamps and marshes. This earned them their moniker.

Of all the compliments paid to marsh tackies, one of the most general yet expansive is that they are an easy-keeping horse. Owners add that they are also easy to train. It has been said of marsh tackies that breaking them can be as simple as sliding a saddle onto their backs.

Unlike high-strung breeds from which they are descended, breeds known to panic when faced with crisis, marsh tackies are fearless, yet they keep their heads and work through confounding circumstances. Their sharp minds make them decisive, and their gentle natures affect level-headed responses to the unexpected.

Their size makes them easy to manage. Averaging thirteen and a half to fifteen hands, they are good fits in the stall, pasture, and trailer. Their colors, consistent with colonial Spanish horses, are dun, bay, blue roan, dun roan, red roan, sorrel, chestnut, black, and grulla. Owners note the sound conformation (structure) of the marsh tacky that allows the equines to work without tiring easily.

As in their earlier utility, they still make good mounts for women and children, thanks to their size and nature. Owners speak of the horses as having a sixth, or "woods" sense, employed instinctively to get them across water obstacles or free from mud when mired. Deer, turkey, and wild boar hunters prize them for their ability to stand their ground unflinchingly when a gun is fired.

Their extinction became a very real possibility in the 1980s and '90s; now their value has been reassessed. Once again, they are being ridden through thickets on hunts for wild boar and deer. They have brought back tradition by racing along stretches of hard-packed beach at low tide. They have shown great promise as endurance or competitive trail horses in the sporting arena.

Through their years in the New World, these equines have handed down—from mare to foal—vital horse sense. Yet humans still are sorting out their mysterious place in history.

CHAPTER ELEVEN

Submerged Mysteries of the Ashley and Cooper Rivers

History scarcely could have hidden its mysteries in better caches than South Carolina tidal swamps and the fickle rivers that flush in and out of them with each changing tide.

At high tide on moonless nights, if legends centuries old can be believed, Edwin Teach uncleated a soggy line holding a low-floating skiff tied up at an unwatched dock and cast off. Obscured by darkness, the bandit would row his way into South Carolina's tidal marsh fingers. The boggy tidal swamps rose and fell with brackish water, first shallow, then deep, as though the marsh itself were breathing in, breathing out.

Marshscapes changing with the light and weather made wayfinding an omnipresent hazard, yet he consulted no map. The certainty of quicksand, along with the coiling infestations of venomous reptiles and the swarming of disease-bearing insects unleashed no fear in the man. In fact, every danger was a pawn in Teach's plan. Nature's forces of defense would keep away curiosity seekers.

There, on islets the scurrilous pirate trusted no one else would have the audacity to approach, he hid treasure stolen on the high seas. Sealed inside sturdy wooden casks were coins, both silver and gold, along with bullion bricks and jewelry he had taken, often at dagger point.

Once satisfied his movements had gone unobserved—at least by human eyes—he poled the lighter-floating skiff back into night as dark as his name. Arrogantly confident, Blackbeard believed his booty would be left undisturbed.

Hiding it well was as exciting to the cutthroat pirate as stealing it had been. No self-respecting pirate could afford to have his stolen booty stolen back. So, safeguarding the buried treasure were some of nature's most pernicious creatures. Poisonous snakes and bloodthirsty mosquitoes, reckoned the brazen buccaneer, would deter even the most tenacious intruder.

Confident he had left nothing to chance, Blackbeard haughtily twirled first one, then the other pig-tailed braid in his thick, black beard. The treasures he had wrested from ships' crews and sojourners on the open waters were deeply hidden. There was more than he could spend in ten lifetimes. Never satisfied, he always went back to sea for more.

Sailing into Charleston's harbors in the eighteenth century, ships likely bore cargoes of rum, sugar, molasses, as well as fruit, gold, and jewels. Goods and precious stuffs were often claimed before they reached their intended destinations. Ruthless pirates, not only Blackbeard but Stede Bonnet as well, regularly lightened the cargo holds of ships along the Atlantic coast.

Years of terrorizing ships' crews and passengers made pirates wealthy, but neither Teach nor Bonnet lived to reclaim their stolen treasures. Since Teach's death, explorers continue to search for his legendary hoard of treasure. To this very day, treasure hunters, armed now not only with shovels but with highly sensitive metal detectors, hope to be the ones discovering in exactly which tidal marsh he buried the stolen treasure.

But every man's treasure is not pirate booty. For many the exhilaration of the search, then the find, then the interpretation and understanding of the discovery is treasure enough. What can be found along the unique Cooper and Ashley River trails is better than margin notes in a well-worn history text.

On a six-mile stretch of the Cooper River, before it flows into the Atlantic Ocean, the South Carolina Institute of Archaeology and Anthropology created perhaps the nation's first underwater archaeological trail. Unlike pirates for whom broadsides and cutlasses were standard operating gear, discoverers zip into second-skin wetsuits and strap on underwater goggles before dropping to the river's bottom to see what treasures it holds.

Known as the remains of colonial plantation sites and old trade routes, the submerged hunting grounds are filled with pottery, old bottles, fossilized sharks' teeth dating in the millions of years, and American mastodon and woolly mammoth bones and teeth, not to mention whale ribs and ear bones. Quite a different kind of treasure, but for state-licensed hobby divers, fair game so long as they report what and where they found it.

The rivers' bottoms and banks are troves of historic treasures from the state's maritime legacies. Whereas Blackbeard and Bonnet left no treasure maps, twenty-first-century heritage hunters, both paddling and diving, follow well-marked, interpretive trails leading them on a chronological timeline of the state's riverine and coastal history. Best of all, the hunting is legal, unlike the barbarous practices of Blackbeard and Bonnet.

Fingers of water encircle these dense marsh islets pirates liked to bury treasure on. Then the brackish water flows back into the two rivers from which they feed. Twin tidal rivers, the Cooper and Ashley, are named for the same Anthony Ashley Cooper, chief Lord Proprietor of the Carolina Colony. The rivers join at the Charleston harbor, a natural geographic feature that lured English settlers to drop anchor in 1670 and name the landing for their king. Proud Charlestonians say, perhaps tongue in cheek, the two rivers join to form the Atlantic Ocean.

The river called Cooper by the early settlers was "Etiwan" to Native Americans.

To forge inroads into the interior of land called Chicora by natives, settlers needed to transport goods and crops—and themselves. Because the Cooper River was navigable for thirty miles or so inland, it attracted many types of watercraft. Commercial and residential development sprung up quietly along both banks.

Carolina settlers searched within their new parameters for commodities to sell to each other, to Europe, and the West Indies. From coastal forests they harvested naval stores: turpentine, pitch, lumber, tar, and staves for barrel-making.

The new port into which the Cooper River flowed was the center of the colony's economy, so relics from it tell a commercial history. For deer and beaver skins, colonists bartered with Indians for trinkets, cloth, and hatchets. South Carolina exported animal pelts to furriers and hat makers throughout Europe.

Although clues to the mysterious demise of myriad submerged relics have been eroding slowly for hundreds of years, there still are secrets to discover. To those who revere history and the rivers, finding these treasures is tantamount to pirates' booty.

Defying buoyancy, a hand-grip of cable at a time, their early descent is illuminated by shards of sunlight glowing through the water. Soon a point is reached at which divers can see neither the surface nor the bottom.

From then on down, the water becomes darker and darker. At depths of thirty-five feet, visibility may be only five or six feet if the tide is coming in. Ebbing tides diminish visibility to as little as one foot, making it essential for divers to be alert for tangles of fishing line left behind by unknowing or careless anglers.

The oldest submerged mystery on the underwater trail is what remains to be seen of old Strawberry Ferry. The ferry landing was built in 1705 to provide crossings between Charleston and the frontier town of Childesbury, on the opposite bank, as well as other outlying settlements.

Established on the Cooper River's western branch early in the eighteenth century, the conveyance venture opened a fluid vein of commerce for vessels, both inland water and open sailing, ranging from simple canoes to barges. Even steamboats docked there, loading and unloading goods and human cargo at a crossroads named for its owner. James Childs based his enterprise on river traffic.

Of the little town where in the early eighteenth century marine supplies such as masts and tar were produced, cattle

South Caroliniana Library, University of South Carolina, Columbia

The Strawberry Ferry, representing river-oriented entrepreneurship in eighteenth-century South Carolina, now reveals its history lessons from the bottom of the Cooper River.

raised, and a brickyard operated, only tiny Strawberry Chapel still stands on dry land. But in the river, clues to the town's early bustle abound.

For his report back to the Commissioners for Trade and Plantations in England, colonial governor James Glen described the scenario this way: "At times it appears the river is a kind of floating market, and we have numbers of canoes, boats, and pet-tyaguas that ply incessantly, bringing down the country produce to town, and returning with such necessaries as are wanted by the planters."

Divers today find the northeast landing in a condition not unlike it was in its early eighteenth-century operative state. On the interior curve of the river, where roots of trees and boun-tiful sawgrass still hold the embankment, the early colonial landing's maritime relics have been protected through years of storms and erosion.

More clues to that period of the colony's history are sub-merged nearby. The Strawberry Wreck has many legends to reveal, even from its obscure site at the bottom of the river. That it was a sailing vessel is clear, but how many masts it carried remains a mystery, primarily because its keelson is missing.

Maritime scholars hypothesize that the small sloop or schooner played a pivotal role in the colony's bid for indepen-dence, because evidence of burning on the timbers ties it con-vincingly to a 1781 raid made by Col. Wade Hampton and his partisans.

The expedition to chase the British out of Moncks Corner came upon a small British warship loaded with local indigo for its return voyage. Small flat-headed copper sheathing tacks with the British broad arrow mark, detected soon after the wreck was discovered, reveal this vessel once belonged to British admiralty.

How was that mystery solved? Naval historians can say with authority that copper sheathing was introduced into the Royal Navy after the mid-1700s. Ships generally were not sheathed with metal until late in the eighteenth century when steam power in mills brought sheet metal into shipbuilding, at least on the better constructed vessels.

Upstream, a sailing ship buried in the sand has become known to discoverers as the Pimlico Wreck. Hefty dimensions and robust scantlings, such as frames and planking, suggest the vessel was crafted for offshore sailing, not inland waterways. Like many vessels pressed into service for multiple purposes, it also may have been used for the lumber trade, commerce, or even warfare.

Settlers needed reliable vessels built for local conditions and quickly realized deep-draft European ships, even ships made of European designs, were impractical in the shallow waters. Sawing planks for small European-style vessels was costly, so colonists learned from Indians how to make dugout crafts from the plentiful bald cypress trees along coastal waterways. Shipbuilder and author William Fleetwood Jr. called the dugout the Model T of colonial ships—"seemingly everywhere and used for every purpose."

How did the Pimlico end up on the bottom of the river? It may have sailed upstream to the "freshes" to flush off marine organisms that attacked the bottoms of wooden ships that had been in salt water. Or could it have sought shelter upriver when a hurricane threatened?

Clues date the ship to the early to mid-nineteenth century. Remains of the vessel's lower hull are discernable from bow to stern. Since it had no ballast stones in its hold, discoverers figure the ship was stripped and abandoned. No other artifacts are present to lend credence to speculation, although the site is littered with aboriginal ceramic ware that may have drifted down from nearby Native American sites. An alternative theory is that the English planned to take samples of Native American pottery back to the mother land for examination. Techniques surviving thousands of years deserve study.

The last two Cooper River underwater trail sites are associated with Henry Laurens, a prominent colonial planter, merchant, ship owner, and politician. First recorded into history in 1681, the three-thousand-acre plantation Laurens founded originally was Native Americans' hunting ground. In 1949 Mepkin Plantation became Mepkin Abbey, a community of Roman Catholic monks of the Abbey of Gethsemani in Kentucky who belong to the worldwide Order of Cistercians of the Strict Observance popularly known as Trappists. A shipwreck, which Laurens's 1766 estate records confirm as his schooner, the *Baker*, is now on the river bottom about twenty-two feet down, listing to the port side at rest on a bed of hard marl. This boat, which Laurens owned until 1827, plied the busy waters between Mepkin, the entrepreneur's plantation, and his wharf in Charleston. Cargo found on board more than a century and a half later included siding planks and a multitude of stoneware jugs that dated the wreck to the early 1800s. The remains of the small sailing vessel, showing evidence of burning, consist of the lower hull, from bow to the mortise of the stern post. Its stern post and rudder are missing from the remains of Laurens's schooner, but, ironically, the rudder was found in the 1970s, more than a century too late to direct the sloop safely back to Laurens's plantation wharf. Letters found among Laurens's papers reveal the sloop was in trouble even before fire befell it. Correspondence between Laurens and his brother James made reference to the vessel's need for repair and, in a subsequent letter, further reference the recommended repair had not corrected the problems.

I have but lately got the Baker out of the Carpenters Hands & now it appears that her bottom is so bad, that it remains a Doubt whether she will swim with a Load of Wood which she is gone to make tryal of. It was the Carpenter's opinion, that to Give her a new Bottom & thorough Repair would be as Expensive as to Build a new Vessel, & besides that she would not have been finish'd for this Season. Therefore I thought it best to Defer that. If it proves unfit for Service, I must endeavor to sell the Wood which is Cut at the Landing.

Like Laurens's, it was not unusual for large plantations to have their own shipyards for vessel construction and repair. Until local labor learned the requisite skills, planters hired European shipwrights, primarily to build sloops and schooners. Because the relatively small vessels were nimble and easy to maneuver, they were ideal for shoal-infested coastal waters.

The landings from which such vessels launched jutted out into maritime history. Adjacent to the plantation landing are submerged remains of a slatted, criblike dock structure. Such structures are excellent clues to past engineering, construction, and craftsmanship practices.

At that eighteenth-century landing, goods and products destined for plantation use or sale in Charleston were loaded and offloaded. Relics of the era scattered about the landing are plantation-made bricks, tiles, ceramics, and miscellaneous iron fasteners.

Other clues to the state's maritime mysteries are a series of anchors left strewn along the river bottom. Relics comprising the anchor farm are all located within close enough proximity to the other underwater landmarks so as to extend the discovery experience.

The centerpiece of the anchor farm collection is a 1,400-pound hunk of metal that once stilled a large vessel whose historical significance, so far, has defied definition. Poachers took the anchor from a wreck along the trail, but downstream. When their theft was brought to justice, a judge offered the two an option: put the weighty anchor back in a secure location or pay a hefty fine and have the theft on your records.

Securing it at an appropriate location along the underwater archaeological trail was a good option, and soon other anchors were moved, or left, to impart their individual clues as to what expeditions or utilitarian tasks they had been part of. A shrimper snagged yet another anchor that soon was positioned in the channel near the first anchor.

Mysteries as to the demise of vessels litter the Ashley riverbanks. The upper reaches of the river were probably a convenient location to scuttle boats that had become unserviceable. Reported historical usage of this river for "hurricane holding" might also account for a high number of damaged and abandoned boats.

Without diving or even getting wet, one can spot historically comparable clues to the state's river-centered beginnings on a float down the contiguous Ashley River. Visible primarily at low tide, the diverse range of wooden sailing crafts, as well as motorized vessels, include a workhorse barge and a tugboat of composite wood and concrete construction. The four-mile floating timeline is punctuated by remains of vessels navigating as early as the plantation era through the post–Civil War years when phosphate mining drove the agrichemical economy.

Within the hulls of two motorized vessels were discovered bountiful phosphate nuggets, tying them to that stage in the state's commercial development. At a time when agriculture in the state needed an economic boost, Charleston "gentlemen scientists" Francis S. Holmes and St. Julien Ravenel, along with chemists N. A. Pratt and C. U. Shepard, solved a long-held mystery. The "sinking stones," so plentiful locally, contained a high bone phosphorous of lime content, very good for soil.

After leading the state, the region, even the world in phosphate production and sales during a critical economy period, the industry fell into obsolescence. Politics, luck, and weather all turned on the industry late in the nineteenth century, often abandoning the vessels that conveyed the sinking stones to market.

These relics from the state's maritime history, like those of the pirates, remain buried. But unlike those stolen by pirates, these submerged artifacts belong to the people of South Carolina for study and appreciation of a time when the natural harbor enabled the colony to lead the American South in maritime trade. After the colony became a state, South Carolina continued its dominance in maritime commerce for many years.

CHAPTER 12

Secrets of the Hunley

Why time and tides did not rust the *Hunley* into oblivion is one of nautical history's great mysteries, but with nature's help, the secrets of the stealthy Confederate submarine remained hidden—in iron—for well over a century.

Capt. George Dixon and his crew of volunteers achieved their mission that cold February night in 1864 when the *Hunley* rammed its explosive-packed torpedo into the iron hull of the USS *Housatonic,* sinking the Union blockade runner in minutes.

But what happened next? Although volunteers on the beach at Sullivan's Island believed they saw the prearranged blue light signal, signifying that a bonfire should be lit to guide the vessel in, the submarine was not seen again, not for well over a century.

Where was it all those years? Author Clive Cussler, an underwater archaeologist who has found numerous Civil War vessels, once said: "Shipwrecks are never where they are supposed to be."

Was it Cussler's team of divers—Ralph Wilbanks, Wes Hall, and Harry Pecorelli—who located the real spot in which the *Hunley* had been at rest all those years? Cussler's early May 1995 announcement that they had found the long-lost *Hunley* resounded around the world.

Or did Dr. C. Lee Spence really figure it out as early as 1970? Spence's published findings were entered into the National Register of Historic Places by the National Park Service two and a half decades before the Cussler announcement.

Each question about the *Hunley* seems to beget yet another question. And as curiosities surface, researchers have not dawdled awaiting definitive answers. Rewarded along the way by new and surprising finds, they have stayed the course toward unraveling the conundrum.

Even after the sunken submarine was found, more than five years of research and exploration elapsed before the vessel, first

IMAGE BY DANIEL DOWDEY/WWW.DOWDEY.COM

The *Hunley* submarine made nautical history as the first to sink an enemy ship in battle—the USS *Housatonic* in Charleston Harbor.

in its nautical class to accomplish its designers' intent, could be brought safely to the surface on August 8, 2000. Since then it has been secured in a specially designed North Charleston facility, the Warren Lasch Conservation Center.

The new century has been rife with discoveries as scientists in multiple disciplines—conservators, archaeologists, even a forensic genealogist—have attempted to unlock the *Hunley*'s sequence of mysteries. Using time-tested hands-on practices as well as cutting-edge technologies, the team has learned from the *Hunley*'s own innovations.

Its enduring mystique can be traced to its days on engineers' drawing tables in New Orleans. Nearly a century and a half after the unexplained disappearance of the first submarine to sink an enemy ship during wartime, the torpedo boat continues to relinquish answers.

Built in secrecy by private investors in a Mobile, Alabama, machine shop as a privateer, or Confederate government-licensed warship, the cunning invention was conceived in patriotic desperation. Its architects, Horace L. Hunley, James McClintock, and Baxter Watson—all knowledgeable about water's physical properties and resistance—were masterminds of pressure for propulsion, and balanced weight for directional force.

The small vessel was tried and tested under two iterations, two names, in two bodies of water before the third and final submarine was cleared to traverse contiguous Confederate states by rail and join the war effort in Charleston, South Carolina's harbor.

First, there had been the *Pioneer,* built for a three-man crew and launched successfully early in 1862 in New Orleans. Its performance buoyed inventors' expectations, leading them to solicit status for it as a privateer, meaning it was authorized by the Confederate government to attack Union vessels.

But as New Orleans was falling into Union hands, the trio of inventors scuttled their beloved vessel in the bay to prevent its detection by the enemy. H. L. Hunley, James McClintock, and Baxter Watson collected as many of their plans and designs as they could manage, and quietly made their way to Mobile, Alabama, a safer port, they believed.

Encouraged by the *Pioneer*'s successful trials that fall, the three men began work anew at Park and Lyon, a Mobile machine shop. In that foundry and fabrication establishment, they met William Alexander, an English-born mechanical engineer who was in Mobile to recast rifle barrels for the Confederate cause.

Soon after the three began on a replacement submarine, Alexander was reassigned to work with them; the submarine took precedence over the rifles. Ultimately, the original designers also met George Dixon, a nautically savvy young lieutenant destined to captain their invention on her triumphant but fatal voyage of February 17, 1864.

Busy readying for secret service a second ship, the *American Diver,* the architects—now joined by Alexander—may not have known that Union naval engineers had recovered the *Pioneer* from Lake Pontchartrain back in New Orleans. Submarine Number

Two was to be a thirty-six-foot-long design update reflecting lessons learned from the initial construction, this time with room to accommodate more machinery and a five-man crew.

That the inventors, backers, captains, and crews believed so fervently, so unswervingly, the vessel could turn the tide of war is one of the most riveting aspects of its valiant, yet tragic legacy.

First, the architects of the vessel, now most notably Alexander, pondered how to make their vessel safe for the crew. That ships of iron could be made to float was a new revelation in that era of naval history. Sections of a former boiler were used for the torpedo boat's hull. How its plates were secured, though, was a modern marvel—for the time. Rivets were countersunk and planed down so the craft could move smoothly through water. Similar welding techniques are used in today's aeronautical industry.

How the vessel could submerge, then regain enough buoyancy to return to the surface with a reversal of mechanisms and human-generated power was choreography that had to work perfectly. The complex pumping system controlled levels in the ballast tanks, provided pressurization, and allowed the crew to monitor levels of water in each tank.

Would water eventually find a way into the hull? Designers wondered, then incorporated an intricate bilge system in hopes of keeping as dry as possible the workplace of a crew that had volunteered to hand-crank the propeller.

Some believe the *American Diver* may also have been an early, if not the first, ship to be propelled by electromagnetic engine. Designer James McClintock referenced, in correspondence he penned following the war, just how much lost time and money had gone into building such an engine for the *American Diver*, the second in the seagoing trio.

The engineers had to be able to generate enough horsepower to achieve the speed necessary for a stealth attack. When the effort to craft such an engine in a reasonable amount of time was unsuccessful, the trio of Louisiana inventors reverted to steam as a more familiar alternative source of power, and for that application, the boiler was innovative.

Scholars close to the research posit the way the craft would have been powered was to amass enough steam while gliding on the water's surface to keep it going for the duration of a mission, the steam's heat source being extinguished in preparation for diving beneath the surface. Such a tactic would have limited how long the submarine could remain under water.

Once designers perfected a vessel that could dive, be propelled underwater, then surface again on demand, the submarine's final requirement was that it be able to sink an enemy ship. The ironclad ships the Union navy was using to blockade Southern harbors necessitated shrewdness. The submarine's designers came up with a barbed spar capable of penetrating an iron hull. The lanyard system to deliver the spar and the explosive mounted onto its tip was another innovation.

Extending less than a foot from the boat's lower bow was a Y-shaped yoke of solid iron; attached to that was an iron pole—the spar—more than seventeen feet long. At the tip of the spar, a simple can of powder fitted with a trigger was the torpedo, a bomb, reputedly packed with at least ninety pounds of gunpowder and, at its tip, a barbed knifelike blade.

If all went as planned, as the spool played out, the rope would tighten, eventually throwing a trigger inside the torpedo that detonated its payload of gunpowder, first giving the torpedo boat ample time and space to move clear of any explosives.

On paper it all worked. Tests and trials on and under water went well. Promise was replaced with reports of the second submarine's demise on Valentine's Day 1863. When the *American Diver* sank in rough seas or perhaps foul weather, Confederate naval officials were not surprised, although it was Mobile Bay's depths that had blunted their confidence. They had surmised that Mobile Bay was too shallow to allow a submerged vessel to navigate beneath the hull of an anchored blockading ship.

During such dire economic times, cost would have been a likely deterrent to a third submarine's fabrication, but before the early architects became discouraged, a corps of patriotic engineers formed in Mobile, the original three as founding members. Incentive to invest in innovations that could spark the war effort had been placed on the table by the Confederate States of America. Members of the recognized investment group, which named themselves the Singer Submarine Corps, would share half the value of any vessels destroyed by an invention emanating from the group.

Well-versed in all aspects of invention and product development, the group was comprised of the submarine's original designers as well as R. W. Dunn, J. D. Breaman, and E. C. Singer, whose uncle had patented the sewing machine shortly before war erupted. In time it was to group member Gus Whitney, a relative of cotton gin inventor Eli Whitney, that Gen. P. T. G. Beauregard telegraphed his fervent message, asking for the submarine to make its way to Charleston. "It is much needed here," wrote the commander of coastal defenses in South Carolina, Georgia, and Florida.

After a series of setbacks and losses, in February 1863 the submarine's operators were being pressured by the Confederacy to make something happen. The Confederate cause sorely needed a win, a victory of morale if not of material damage. In the short history of the submarine, General Beauregard had doubted, then later gambled it could be the secret weapon that could change the war's course.

The Confederacy's hope for a way to blast through that blockade had rolled undetected across the South on two flatbed rail cars, its dead-giveaway shape disguised under yards of dark tarpaulin. The submarine's clandestine maneuvers had just begun.

The *Hunley* arrived August 12, 1863, covertly entering the city where the first shots of the war had been fired, a city whose port was blockaded by Union ships. Shipments of needed goods, originating in Europe and the Caribbean Islands, sent by sympathetic businessmen, were not allowed to be offloaded. People in the South, especially in cities, were suffering. The nautical stranglehold manifested President Abraham Lincoln's Anaconda Plan: to blockade all Southern ports from Virginia to Texas.

In Charleston and its surrounds, the vessel continued to be in much danger of detection. The federals' presence, swinging at anchor in Charleston Harbor, made it hazardous for the crew to go about its training during daylight hours.

Deflecting attention away from the submarine, considered a formidable weapon by the Confederacy, were nimble little crafts known as Davids. Why Davids? Their name was borrowed from the diminutive David who took down Goliath.

The Davids' presence in and around Sullivan's Island may have accustomed those in the area to seeing cigar-shaped vessels in those waters. Davids were considered fairly benign, even after one attacked the *New Ironsides*. Although the hit failed to sink one of the Union's original three ironclad warships, it lifted Confederate morale—briefly.

When the Union Army's Swamp Angel, a siege cannon newly introduced into warfare, fired into Charleston from Morris Island, the need for retaliation intensified. Confederate leaders wanted their own secret weapon to move into action, and when the privateer's Singer crew continued training, watching and waiting for an optimum opportunity, they were summarily written off as ineffective. The Confederate government seized the vessel, dismissed the Singer crew, and quickly gave the command to naval veteran Lt. John Payne.

Whereas the Singer crew had undertaken both day and nocturnal training, Payne put his crew through its paces only during daylight hours—as crowds gathered on shore to watch the rehearsals. Only days after Payne assumed command, the *Hunley* sank just off the docks at Fort Johnson, taking down five of nine crewmen. Payne and the others escaped and swam to shore.

Could the vessel's mechanical simplicity have lulled the new captain and volunteer crew into complacency? With each subsequent design, the submarine's function was simplified, even though sophisticated applications were employed.

There are different versions of what caused the accident, but at least one eyewitness said Payne accidentally tripped, or stepped on a lever that controlled the two diving planes, leaving the hatches open at the wrong time. Another account relates that a friendly ship passed by when the hatches were open, its wake swamping the *Hunley.*

Impetus to bring the "fish boat," as the vessel was called, up from the bottom extended beyond the need of final rites for the five lost crewmen, or even the need to get the ship back into the war game, although that was a high priority. There was fear that the Union would somehow recover the innovation and turn it against its developers. When it was raised and cleaned, its equipment was repaired. Payne was given another try, but again, before the boat even got away from the dock, it was swamped again.

Fourteen, so far, had given their lives to the pioneering venture. So, how were captains of the submarine able to recruit new volunteer crews? Finally, General Beauregard called on H. L. Hunley.

Hunley knew the submarine, as he had its two predecessors, inside and out, and his opinion held considerable weight when he recommended to General Beauregard that Lieutenant George Dixon step up as captain. But in October 1863, Dixon was mysteriously back in Mobile with James McClintock where the two, attached to a Confederate unit, continued other important work, perhaps working on munitions, perhaps on underwater obstructions.

Hunley's other duties, some say as a secret agent for the Confederacy, had kept him away from the vessel for periods of time. He may have lost some of his intimate familiarity with the craft, but he was present and accounted for on October 15 for a mock attack staged in the Charleston Harbor. Although it had logged a number of successful dives, the submarine failed to resurface after a practice run under the Confederate vessel *Indian Chief.* That failed mission took Hunley, along with the rest of the crew, to a watery grave. Casualties now numbered twenty-three.

But once again, the Confederacy salvaged the boat, although General Beauregard immediately ordered the *Hunley* be used no further as a submerged boat. It would remain in service but be relegated to a role much like the Davids. But he relented when Lt. George Dixon made his ardent case for allowing him to captain the ship. Dixon, more determined than ever to honor the lead inventor and backer's memory by taking out an enemy ship, was diligent in his preparation of the latest crew to volunteer.

Even before the *Hunley* took its dive into history on February 17, 1864, the mysteries were mounting. Was Dixon's crew really ready for an offensive, or were they being pushed to move too soon by Confederates desperate for a breakthrough? And why was McClintock still in Mobile, not with the submarine into which he had poured so much careful thought, design, and work? He would have been on that crew if not ordered to complete some project in Alabama.

Union Admiral John Dahlgren had been tipped off about the threat posed by the wonder-boat. Two deserters had seen the craft in Mobile with their own eyes; they got most of the facts correct. So to counter potential attacks, the commander of the blockading fleet off Charleston issued a warning and a set of orders.

Ships were not to remain static in the harbor; they should be stoked and in motion at all times on the chance they should need to get away quickly. They were to anchor a good distance away from each other and in water too shallow for a stealthy vessel to navigate under them. Ironclads were not to have their fenders rigged out; guns were to be loaded and aimed.

Dahlgren, himself an inventor—of the smooth bore cannon—also ordered ships to drop a net down to protect their hulls. On the fateful night, the USS *Housatonic* was not in compliance with this last order. Anchored several miles out, and on active watch, the blockade runner was relying only on its duty watch to note anything unusual. The *Hunley* easily torpedoed its barbed spar into the sloop of war's hull, sinking the enemy ship in minutes. This was a first for a submarine.

But what happened next? Volunteers watching from Sullivan's Island were certain they saw the blue light signal emanate from the submarine just minutes after the explosion that removed the Union's lead ship from the fleet. As soon as they saw that light, they were to light a bonfire on the beach, a beacon by which the captain would navigate the vessel in. The volunteers kept the fire burning all night, throwing on dry driftwood when the blaze died down, but by morning the *Hunley* had not surfaced, had not landed.

For well over a century, historians have pondered what went wrong. How could the *Hunley* have achieved its military objective, signaled it was heading to shore, then disappeared? They ponder still.

Of all the *Hunley* mysteries still unsolved or legends that have surfaced in the last decade, one of the most titillating was discovered not in the Charleston Harbor but more than a hundred miles inland. An interior swamp cut through by a railroad bed may have held on to its secrets for nearly as many years as Charleston Harbor cradled the sunken submarine on its sandy bottom.

Hobby archaeologists tromping through the Wateree Swamp, assessing the havoc wreaked by Hurricane Hugo in 1989, unearthed the splintered vestige of a wooden box. Considering how deeply the box was imbedded into the side of the trestle, the explorers supposed the military-looking crate had been imploded into the dark soil.

Inside the box's remains were glass test tubes. With no way of knowing what they had stumbled upon, the explorers removed one of the test tubes with great care. As they held the soil-coated test tube up to the dappled light filtering through the swamp's green canopy, they could see that inside was another vial.

Within that vial, hermetically sealed by a wad of dingy cotton, was a clear-colored fluid, still viscous after an unknown number of decades. At first blush the two men suspected the encased elixir might have been the anesthetic chloroform because of the small amount suspended in each cylinder.

But their knowledge of the area's history soon had them thinking differently. During the Civil War, those tracks—obscured by the swamp and the dense forest thriving within it—had been the rail path along which boxcars bearing munitions lumbered toward Confederate strongholds under heavy guard and cover of darkness. After further speculation the two explorers deduced the care with which the vials were packed suggested explosives.

Sumter, the town closest to the vials' discovery, was a center for Confederate stores and munitions. Slowly, the clues began adding up. The intrepid duo pieced together other historic facts and a picture began to emerge. Sure, the munitions trains the two had read and heard about had cut as quiet a swath as possible through the South. They recalled that rails had been the effective way of getting munitions to Atlanta, the Confederacy's munitions distribution hub.

If the vials did contain explosives, were they something new Southern strategists hoped would prove advantageous to the war effort? What special plans were interrupted by the accident that sent the wooden crate careening into the railroad bank? Suddenly, the two men thought about nitroglycerin, a widely used explosive in the nineteenth century. They knew even a small vibration could set off an explosion. Could an explosion have come from inside the railcar, not from enemy troops intent on preventing the train from making its delivery?

Well documented in history were all sorts of technological cunning and medical advancements, rushed to theaters of operations in hopes of a gained advantage. Could the small amount of liquid—secured in a vial no longer than two inches, with a diameter of only about a half-inch—bring about an explosion powerful enough to penetrate, say, the hull of an ironclad ship?

If so, could one of the material's intentions have been to blast through the Union forces' nautical blockade in Charleston Harbor, a hundred miles to the east? Could those explosives have altered the *Hunley*'s fate? The bounty the Confederacy placed on sinking one of those vessels surely would have inspired a lot of courage and ingenuity.

As train cars loaded with munitions made their way haltingly through the Carolinas, stopping to offload needed supplies before reaching their Atlanta terminus, another race was underway. A nautical experiment, a submarine named the *Hunley*, lurked in the shallows about four miles from Breach Inlet. Its captain and crew counted on the currents to remain calm, and for its target of the night, the USS *Housatonic,* to remain in its anchored position.

That fateful night, the *Hunley*'s torpedo spar was packed with at least ninety pounds of fine grain black powder. If a far lighter explosive had been available, one that was equally as effective, or even more potent, could the spar have been lengthened a few extra inches? Would a lighter-weight explosive, or a slightly longer spar, have bought the submarine a couple of seconds more to back itself into a safer range after ramming its target?

As is often the case with mysteries, this one cannot be proven. From the early stages of its design, the submarine's trio of backers and inventors knew the innovation had to do far more than be new and different. Without the ability to blow up and sink an enemy ship, history might describe the diver as stealthy, but would not ascribe to the *Hunley* the desired designation: weapon.

The two men subjected a sample of their find to a twentieth-century chemical test, undertaken in a controlled university laboratory setting. The university chemist determined the mysterious viscous material was not nitroglycerin but concentrated sulfuric acid. Such a chemical would have been an ideal fuse because it could be handled with confidence but would explode quickly upon contact with any substance.

It is possible the highly explosive matter found embedded beneath a trestle in the Wateree Swamp was destined for Charleston where it would have been mounted into the hollow end of a torpedo spar. Upon contact the waterproof interior glass tube would have broken, exposing sulfuric acid to an exact measure of chlorate of potash and sugar, setting off an immediate explosion.

The *Hunley*'s target that cold February evening was the two-hundred-foot-long steam- and sail-powered USS *Housatonic* in position in twenty-eight feet of water in the North Channel opposite Breach Inlet. The sailor on watch first thought what he saw in the water was a log. But it was moving directly toward the sloop of war.

In response to the sailor's call out, the deck filled immediately with Union soldiers who attempted to halt with rifle shots whatever was in the water. But too much planning, too many dress rehearsals had readied the *Hunley* crew for that fateful mission. The spar torpedo rammed into the hull of the *Housatonic* and, upon impact, an explosion tore through the iron side. In less than five minutes, the ship went under, sailors clinging to its three masts until they could be rescued, as nearly all of them were.

Yet the *Hunley* crew did not return. Why? Theories abound. Did the sinking *Housatonic* somehow trap the *Hunley* in its vortex?

Even the best efforts by the most specialized researchers working in the field may never fully solve all the mysteries of the *Hunley*.

CHAPTER THIRTEEN

Digging for Timelines

Running one hand along a sprawling outcropping of flint-like rock, his other hand shading his eyes for a glimpse of the Savannah River's nearby curve, Dr. Al Goodyear had never been so glad to be wrong.

Unaided, it is unlikely Goodyear ever would have found the spot that, for Early Man, was a veritable hardware store—because he would not have looked. His colleagues at the South Carolina Institute of Archaeology and Anthropology believed there was but one flint—or chert—outcropping along the South Carolina side of the Savannah River. He had believed it too.

But some time after avocational archaeologist David Topper reiterated his willingness to show the research professor there was more than one exposed chert site on the river, Goodyear capitulated. With chert on his mind, one day in 1981 the professor picked up the phone and called the forester. When he met Topper at an Allendale restaurant for the dirt-road rumble over to the site, Goodyear put his assumptions in neutral and prepared for the possibility of having at least one theory overturned. Deep on a tract of private land then owned by Sandoz Chemical Corporation, the beautiful setting was a bluff above the Savannah River, five hundred feet from its main branch. A soft breeze was blowing. In his mind Goodyear time-traveled back thousands of years and figured, sure, if I were Early Man, this is where I would want to be.

A mild climate, a river representing sources of water and food, not to mention transportation—it was all there. Then there was the chert. An easy-flaking sedimentary rock that can be chipped and shaped to make tools such as knives, arrows, axes, and blades, chert, especially in such massive outcroppings, frequently corresponds to the presence of Early Man.

It took time for Goodyear to obtain the necessary permissions to search and excavate on corporate land and to raise funds for the project. There were samples to take, preliminary studies to make, equipment to requisition, and help to assemble. By 1984 Goodyear began digging at the ancient chert quarry site outside Allendale that he named for the man who led him to it.

From 1984 to 1994, as Goodyear searched for Paleoindian evidence, every new find further substantiated that the chert site and surroundings had been, for those first to discover it, a manufacturing center, complete with its own supply of raw materials for making all kinds of tools. But how long had the site been used for toolmaking? And, over thousands of years, how had these early people communicated that this location was the place to come make their tool kits?

Ignited by early findings, and how they were rewriting history, Goodyear's infectious enthusiasm spilled over. By 1996 the curious had signed on as volunteers, and working at the Allendale Paleoindian Expedition, as it then was being called, had become a late spring ritual among a growing network of avocational archaeologists. Word spread that you could come to Allendale County and have an exciting, hands-on learning experience. Goodyear's solid academic reputation drew professional peers as well and, in the evenings when top scholars and researchers gave informal after-dinner talks, volunteers were mesmerized.

Since the 1930s scientists had believed the New World's first human inhabitants were the Clovis people. Thought to have followed large game across the Bering Sea land bridge, the Clovis made their way to most parts of the present United States and as far south as Panama. They were so named because first evidence of their presence on this continent was found at Clovis, New Mexico. In 1998 spring floods on the Savannah River forced the expedition from its tried and true Big Pine Tree site where 13,000-year-old stone material dating to the Clovis period had been found consistently during other field seasons. But there Goodyear was, a team of volunteers signed up, eager to dig, and the site on which he could usually count on their hitting Clovis "paydirt" was swamped.

The expedition director's reluctant second choice as a dig spot was the outcropping bearing the name of the man who first showed him the site. To the leader Topper seemed like just a chert quarry, yet it was high above the raging floods of the Savannah River. Once Goodyear acquiesced to the idea of moving that season's dig over to Topper, a lightbulb came on.

He thought about recent discoveries made in Monte Verde, Chile, and Cactus Hill, Virginia. Just a year earlier, excavators had dug deeper than the science-accepted forty meters and found artifacts test-dated at 14,000 years old—making the people who left them there pre-Clovis people. The landform at Topper suggested that, if someone had been there before Clovis, then artifacts might be buried down deeper.

How daunting it would be not to find anything at that level, the professor mused. Even more daunting—what if the excavators actually found something below Clovis! Like most students the genial archaeologist had learned in his formative history classes, and perpetuated in his college teachings, that Ice Age hunters entered Alaska from Siberia 13,000 years ago.

If something left behind by man even earlier than that were found, Goodyear would have to re-evaluate everything he thought he knew. And his professional peers would clamor for indisputable proof. He asked the team, many of whom had taken vacation time and traveled long distances to work on this dig, if they wanted to dig deeper. Their leader was not disappointed when they found nothing for the first foot and a half. Every excavation does not yield a harvest of artifacts.

Then team members began finding small flakes and microtools, evidence man had been in South Carolina earlier than anyone had anticipated. Intrigued to learn more, Goodyear nervously held evidence in his hand, knowing full well an announcement that pre-Clovis findings had been unearthed in Allendale would raise academic eyebrows.

The 1998 discovery that man had worked on tool kits at least 14,000 years ago tipped off the national media, who began covering the site. For the 1999 expedition, highly respected outside archaeologists and geologists were invited in to see for themselves, something of a hands-on peer review. Testing takes time, but by the following field season, consultants confirmed the presence of Ice Age soil, validating the antiquity of the pre-Clovis artifacts.

In 2001 tests dated the pre-Clovis material to at least 14,000 years or older.

To top that, the following year geologists found ancient soil that test-dated to between 16,000 and 20,000 years old.

No findings indicated Clovis or pre-Clovis people lived at the Allendale site for any length of time, only that they came there for toolmaking materials, and obviously worked on them on site as well. Goodyear told volunteers the points and other tools they were finding were the cast-offs, the mistakes. The best razor-sharp stone blades would have been used as knives, arrows, and axes and would have left the area with the hunters.

Each year anticipation of significant new Clovis and pre-Clovis finds kept both volunteers and visiting professionals returning to see what mysteries would be discovered next.

In 2004 deeper excavations unearthed a black stain in the Pleistocene terrace soil. The structural source of that charcoal stain resembled a hearth, or fire pit. An abundant charcoal sample present in the stain told Goodyear the team finally had material on which researchers could attempt radio-carbon dating.

Months after the camp folded that spring, the radio-carbon dating came back indicating humans' arrival in this hemisphere more than 30,000 years earlier than

SCIAA PHOTO BY DARYL P. MILLER

Dr. Al Goodyear stands in an excavated pit where evidence of Clovis and pre-Clovis people have been found.

previously believed. Knowing the reported discovery—50,000 years old—would inspire controversy, Goodyear and his colleagues organized a professional conference, Clovis in the Southeast, to be held in Columbia, making their findings transparent to their peers and giving them context by presenting them alongside other evidence and theories.

One presentation at that conference offered an alternate theory as to how the hemisphere's first humans arrived. Dr. Dennis Stanford, the Smithsonian Institution's curator of archaeology, often a visiting professional at the Topper site, theorized that pre-Clovis people entered the East Coast of North America, and became Clovis people later. From Iberia, not Siberia, argued Stanford, Early Man migrated by boat along the edge of ice sheets in pursuit of marine mammals and fish. Once across the Atlantic Ocean, over significantly lower sea levels and an ice bridge that connected New England to Europe, Stanford and others believe these people arrived on the northeastern coast, then radiated west and south to colonize North America.

To build support for the Solutrean Theory, as that theory is known, Stanford mustered evidence, including a distinctive zigzag pattern on an organic tool found in Florida by C. Andrew Hemmings of the University of Texas, and on a comparable tool from France's Solutrean culture. Was it possible humans could have made it to the New World at about the same time tested evidence had them moving into Europe? Artifacts have placed their presence at myriad sites around the continent—at close to the same time. How had these early inhabitants radiated out to so many North American locations within such a short span of time? It is one of the mysteries yet unsolved. The mystery of the peopling of the Americas was turning out to be more complex than previously thought.

Interest in the Topper site escalated after the conference. Expansions of excavation sites marked the next few years. By now the science media had Allendale on its radar. Coverage was published not only in professional journals but in respected news magazines as well. Science writers sent by publications such as *U.S. News and World Report, Newsweek, National Geographic,* the *New York Times, Scientific American,* and *Science* have had boots on the ground walked by man at least 50,000 years ago. Footage recorded at the site has been broadcast worldwide by CNN and the History Channel, as well as the first one-hour program devoted to Topper produced by Time Team America.

To accommodate growing interest, the expedition's corporate host, Swiss-based Clariant Corporation, which now owns the property on which the site is located, offered private resources for construction of a covered wooden pavilion in 2006. Designed to jut out over the deepening primary excavation site, the pavilion is a vantage point from which visitors—including members of the news media—can look down into the pit; it also helps keep the site dry. With the dedication of this improvement in fall 2006, volunteers in spring 2007 and beyond were able to continue working, even in the rain.

Every year something new was found, often expanding the prior year's defining evidence—and tackling another mystery. For instance, how does science explain the evidence pre-Clovis and Clovis people were there—and then gone? Geoscientists suggest a massive comet exploded around 12,900 years ago above the Great Lakes, raining fiery fragments over North America. It is widely believed the cosmic event returned the Northern Hemisphere to another Ice Age.

The thousand-year environmental aftermath of the Younger-Dryas Event, as it is called, wiped out large beasts—mammoths and mastodons—and greatly diminished the human population around that time. What makes scientists think the event was cosmic, or extraterrestrial? And what does it have to do with the Topper site?

According to Arizona geophysicist Dr. Allen West, evidence the comet catastrophe left behind includes nanodiamonds. Smaller than bacteria, nanodiamonds are invisible except under the lenses of high-powered microscopes. Other than an extraterrestrial event, no natural function produces them. West, since 2005 a regular guest at the Topper site, began examining Clovis sites around the country and found similar materials—nanodiamonds and magnetic microspherules—in Arizona, New Mexico, Oklahoma, and Canada, off the California coast, as well as at Topper. He wanted to learn how the Clovis people would have been impacted by the comet catastrophe.

West's baseline evidence got Goodyear thinking. The research professor went back and re-examined South Carolina's paleopoint database and, lo and behold, he found the occurrence of fluted Clovis spear points dropped off significantly—four to one—after the date assigned to the explosion. For there to be such a significantly lower number of points in the database indicates to scientists there may have been far fewer people shaping those points a century after the last Ice Age.

What else would have wiped out the animals? Disease? Overkilling of food sources—the beasts—by the Clovis people had been speculated, and overchilling by the onset of the Younger-Dryas Ice Age also had been considered, but the comet evidence explained far more.

Material the Arizona geophysicist collected near Allendale further established the Topper site as an important scientific source, and the location has continued to yield new pieces of a great puzzle. Each time a mystery seems to be solving itself, another is suggested.

Scientists and volunteers alike realize there is still much to be discovered about those who came long, long before us.

BIBLIOGRAPHY

One Mine, Three Centuries

Culvern, Julian Brewer. "Going for the Gold at Haile's Gold Mine," *Sandlapper,* Winter 2006–2007.

Edgar, Walter, ed. *The South Carolina Encyclopedia.* Columbia, University of South Carolina Press, 2006.

Haile, Dr. Cantey. Columbia, SC. Personal communication, 2010.

Jameson, W. C. "The Indian Gold Mine de Soto Never Found," in *Buried Treasures of the South.* Little Rock, August House Publishing, Inc., 1992.

Pittman, Clyde C. *Death of a Gold Mine.* Great Falls, SC, self-published, 1972.

South Carolina Museum Commission News, Vol. 5, No. 1, Winter 1979.

Redfern's Last Flight

Gould, James. St. Simon Island, GA. Personal communication, 2009.

Maxey, Russell. *Airports of Columbia.* Columbia, SC, Palmetto Publishing Company, 1987.

Savage, Tom. Paul Rinaldo Redfern Society, Columbia, SC. Personal communication, 2010.

Shelton, Ron. Columbia, SC. Personal communication, 2009.

www.eaa242.org/PaulRefern/redfern_001.asp

Nature's Light Show

Cross, Robert. "Old trees, new title," *Chicago Tribune,* May 9, 2004.

Mancke, Rudy (producer), "Congaree Swamp National Monument," *Nature Scene,* South Carolina Educational Television, 1987.

Newman, Betsy. "Roots in the River," South Carolina Educational Television, 2009.

Rametta, Fran. Interpretive naturalist, Congaree National Park. Columbia, SC. Personal communication, 2009–2010.

www.kadamsphoto.com/nature_recreation/fireflies_lightning_ bugs.htm

www.nationalparkstraveler.com

www.suite101.com/content/synchronized-fireflies-a125124

The Tunnel and the Railroad

Brown, George Dewitt. "A History of the Blue Ridge Railroad, 1852–1874." Master's thesis, University of South Carolina, 1967.

Edgar, Walter, ed. *The South Carolina Encyclopedia*. Columbia, University of South Carolina Press, 2006.

Haughey, Jim. "Tunnel Hill: An Irish Mining Community in the Western Carolinas," *Proceedings of the South Carolina Historical Association* (2004): 51–62.

Plisco, Betty. *The Rocky Road to Nowhere: A History of the Blue Ridge Railroad in South Carolina, 1850–1861*. Salem, SC, Blue Granite Books, 2002.

Legendary White Lines

Daso, Dik Alan. *Doolittle: Aerospace Visionary*. Washington, DC, Brassey's, Inc., 2003.

Glines, Carroll V. *The Doolittle Raid*. West Chester, PA, Schiffer Military History, 1991.

Maxey, Russell. *Airports of Columbia.* Columbia, SC, Palmetto Publishing Company, 1987.

Nelson, Craig. *The First Heroes.* New York, The Penguin Group, 2002.

Reynolds, Quentin. *The Amazing Mr. Doolittle.* New York, Appleton-Century-Crafts, Inc., 1953.

Schulz, Duane. *The Doolittle Raid.* New York, St. Martin's Press, 1988.

Thomas, Lowell and Edward Jablonski. *Doolittle: A Biography.* New York, Doubleday and Company, Inc., 1976.

Carolina Silver in the South Pacific

Andrew, Rod, Jr. *Wade Hampton: Confederate Warrior to Southern Redeemer.* Chapel Hill, University of North Carolina Press, 2008.

Bowman, Janice. Volunteer, Historic Columbia Foundation, Columbia, SC. Personal communication, 2010.

Clarke, Walker. President emeritus, South Carolina Archives and History Foundation, Columbia, SC. Personal communication, 2010.

Durham, Kay. Founding member, South Carolina Silver Society, Columbia, SC. Personal communication, 2010.

Edgar, Walter, ed. *The South Carolina Encyclopedia.* Columbia, University of South Carolina Press, 2006.

Fletcher, Frank. Pawleys Island, SC. Personal communication, 2010.

Maynard, Virginia. *The Venturers.* Greenville, SC, Southern Historical Press, Inc., 1981, 1991.

South Carolina and Confederate Gold

Clancy, W. Power, "Confederate Finance and Supply," Cincinnati Civil War Round Table, February 9, 1961.

Davis, Burke. *The Long Surrender.* New York, Random House, 1985.

Gaines, W. Craig, "Civil War Gold and Other Lost Treasures." Rense.com/general133/civil.htm.

Hanna, A. J. *Flight into Oblivion.* Richmond, VA, Johnson Publishing Company, 1938.

Kuenzi, Hans. "The Search for Lost Confederate Gold," Cleveland Civil War Roundtable, 2008.

Nepveux, Ethel Trenholm Seabrook. *George A. Trenholm: Financial Genius of the Confederacy, His Associates and His Ships That Ran the Blockade.* Anderson, SC, The Electric City Printing Company, 1999.

Shuler, Kristina A., and Ralph Bailey Jr. "The History of Phosphate Mining Industry in the South Carolina Low Country". Brockington and Associates, Mt. Pleasant, SC, 2004.

Wolf, Elizabeth Huntsinger. *Georgetown Mysteries and Legends.* Winston-Salem, NC, John F. Blair, 2007.

Mars Bluff's Atomic Bomb

Dittrick, Luke, "A Perfectly Understandable Mistake," *Esquire,* Vol. 143, Issue 5, May 2005.

Horton, Tom. "An Atom Bomb Fell on Mars Bluff March 11, 1958." www.moultrienews.com. March 2, 2010.

Kirkland, Tom. Florence, SC. Personal communication, 2010.

Yarborough, Marshall. Chairman, Florence City-County Historical Commission. Florence, SC. Personal communication, 2010.

Civil War Graffiti

Conservation report for Lancaster County Courthouse, SC, Crawford Conservation, Inc. July 22, 2009.

Côté, Richard. "Jewel of the Cotton Fields: A History of Secessionville Manor, a Nineteenth-century Summer House on James Island," Charleston County, SC, commissioned report. 1995.

Earnshaw, Tecla and Bruce. Cassina Point, Edisto Island, South Carolina. Personal communication, 2010

Emmons, Karen. Historic Charleston Foundation. Personal communication, 2010.

en.wikipedia.org/wiki/Hugh_Judson_Kilpatrick

Haile, Dr. E. Cantey. Columbia, SC. Personal communication, 2010.

McKown, Bryan. South Carolina Department of Archives and History. Personal communication, 2010.

Spencer, Charles. *Edisto Island, 1861–2006: Ruin, Recovery and Rebirth.* Charleston, SC, The History Press, 2008.

Hoofprints through History

Beranger, Jeanette. American Livestock Breed Conservancy. Personal communication, 2010.

Dutson, Judith. *Storey's Illustrated Guide to 96 Horse Breeds of North America.* North Adams, MA, Storey Publishing, 2005.

Fos, Cassie. "Marsh Tackies Thrill Crowd in Hilton Head Beach Race," *The Island Packet* (Hilton Head, SC), March 1, 2010.

Grant, David. Florence, SC. Personal communication. 2010.

Walsh, Sandra. "Marsh Tackies Not Mere Lore," *Beaufort Gazette* (Beaufort, SC), July 3, 2005.

www.coastaldiscovery.org/marsh

www.marshtacky.org/History-of-theBreed.php

Submerged Mysteries of the Ashley and Cooper Rivers

Amer, Christopher F. State Underwater Archaeologist, Maritime Research Division, South Carolina Institute of Archaeology and Anthropology, University of South Carolina, Columbia, SC, Personal communication, 2010.

Hamer, Philip M. and George C. Rogers, eds. "The Papers of Henry Laurens," Vol. 9, p. 183, South Carolina Historical Society. 1970, 1972.

Hicks, Brian. "Anchor Farm Grows in Cooper," *The Post and Courier* (Charleston, SC), September 14, 2009.

"Rise and Fall and Rise: South Carolina's Maritime History," *Coastal Heritage,* Vol. 17, No. 2, Fall 2002.

Spirek, James and Lynn Harris. "Maritime Heritage on Display: Underwater Examples from South Carolina," *Submerged Cultural Resource Management,* Kluwer Academic/ Plenum Publishers, NY, 2003.

Vezeau, Susan Lynn. "The Mepkin Abbey Shipwreck: Diving into Mepkin Plantation's Past," Texas A&M University, Department of Anthropology, August, 2004.

Wolf, Elizabeth Huntsinger. *Georgetown Mysteries and Legends.* Winston-Salem, NC, John F. Blair, 2007.

Secrets of the *Hunley*

Chaffin, Tom. *The H.L. Hunley: The Secret Hope of the Confederacy.* New York, Hill and Wang, 2008.

Haile, Dr. E. Cantey. "Civil War History in the Wateree Swamp," *Caroliniana Columns,* University of South Carolina, Columbia, SC, Spring 1998.

Hawk, Fran, and Dan Nance, illustrator. *The Story of the H.L. Hunley and Queenie's Coin.* Mt. Pleasant, SC, Sleeping Bear Press, 2004.

Hicks, Brian and Schuyler Kropf. *Raising the Hunley: The Remarkable History and Recovery of the Lost Confederate Submarine,* Waterville, ME, Thorndike Press, 2002.

Smith, Derek. *The Sentinels.* Savannah, GA, Frederic C. Bell, Publishers, Inc., 2001.

Teaster, Gerald. *The Confederate Submarine H.L. Hunley.* Summerville, SC, Junior History Press, 1989.

The Blue Light, various issues. Charleston, SC, Fall 2001– Fall 2007.

Digging for Timelines

Aiken, Ron. "Al Goodyear and the Secrets of the Ancient Americans." *Free Time*, (Columbia, SC), May 14–20, 2008.

"Clovis in the Southeast Conference 2005," *Mammoth Trumpet,* Center for the Study of the First Americans, Texas A&M University, Vol. 21, No. 2, March 2006.

en.wikipedia.org/wiki/Topper_(archaeological_site).

Goodyear, Dr. Albert C. "Update on Research at the Topper Site," *Legacy,* Vol. 13, No. 1, March 2009.

Goodyear, Dr. Albert C. III. Personal communication, 2010.

Mitchell, Liz. "Topper Dig Is Becoming a Renowned Archaeological Treasure Trove," *Island Packet* (Hilton Head, SC), June 27, 2009.

Rose, Mark. "The Topper Site: Pre-Clovis Surprise," *Archaeology Newsbriefs,* Vol. 52, No. 4, July/August 1999.

Toner, Mike. "Impossibly Old America?" *Archaeology Abstracts*, Vol. 59, No. 3, May/June 2006.

Topper, David. Personal communication, 2010.

www.allendale-expedition.net.

www.archaeology.org/0605/abstracts/america.html.

www.sciencedaily.com/releases/2004.

INDEX

ABOUT THE AUTHOR

Rachel Haynie writes about history, interesting characters, and art. She is the author of "Stalled," a nonfiction tale of an Oregon couple's World War II honeymoon in Columbia, South Carolina. Haynie also authored *First You Explore,* a youth-oriented biography of laser pioneer Charles Townes, a South Carolina native. She is based in Columbia.